D0849892

Supplement to Torrey

SUPPLEMENT TO TORREY'S
New England Marriages Prior to 1700

Melinde Lutz Sanborn

Copyright © 1991
Genealogical Publishing Co., Inc.
1001 N. Calvert Street
Baltimore, MD 21202
All Rights Reserved
Library of Congress Catalogue Card Number 91-70357
International Standard Book Number 0-8063-1306-4
Made in the United States of America

For John,

who would have done this

if he had been given the time.

PREFACE

There are many "big" projects left to be done in New England genealogy, and an update to Torrey is high on the list. This small beginning owes sincere thanks to a number of people who were encouraging and supportive. First, to the many researchers who freely offered their opinions and discoveries: Robert Charles Anderson, F.A.S.G., David Curtis Dearborn, F.A.S.G., Jane Fletcher Fiske, F.A.S.G., Henry B. Hoff, F.A.S.G., Ann Smith Lainhart, Andrew B.W. MacEwen, John Hollister McCallum, Julie Helen Otto, George Freeman Sanborn Jr., William H. Schoeffler, Ruth Wilder Sherman, F.A.S.G., and Dean Crawford Smith.

Gary Boyd Roberts of the New England Historic Genealogical Society gave the idea its original impetus, and the boundless patience of Genealogical Publishing Company's Dr. Joseph Garonzik has at last been rewarded.

M.L.S.
Derry, NH
January 1991

INTRODUCTION

When Clarence Almon Torrey died in 1962, his manuscript, New England Marriages Before 1700, was the single best index to the early Colonial Period in existence. Even today, there is nothing like it for both thoroughness and utility. Over a period of more than forty years, Torrey combed the printed collection at the New England Historic Genealogical Society, extracting almost every available reference to marriages of early New England settlers. Only a few of his references came from the Society's considerable manuscript collections, and an even smaller number of citations came from items outside its holdings. Still, it was an extraordinary undertaking, and estimates that it covers almost 99% of the married couples in New England before 1700 are not far off. Among his entries were discoveries not yet in print, showing that he was in close communication with the leading researchers of the day, who, like their present counterparts, are generally open and generous with the results of their investigations.

Despite its great popularity and very frequent use, most people do not appear to understand what it is that Torrey did. Some insist on using Torrey as a reference, when his work is in actuality an *index* to references. Clarence Torrey did not perform the research which determined his entries; his work was a faithful index of what others discovered and published. Thus, his index contains many entries that are incorrect or contradictory; it remains for the user of the index to evaluate the references cited.

The idea of updating Torrey's work has been around for many years. Quite a number of respected names in the genealogical field have considered the idea, even to the extent of beginning the project, starting the systematic search through new material and amassing considerable numbers of files. One and all, these projects have fallen by the wayside, partially because the genealogical publishing phenomenon has geometrically increased the available material, and partially because, to be absolutely complete, it would be necessary to re-examine more than two

9

hundred years of work which Torrey already treated, just to correct a few interpretations and to pick up a few missed entries.

The present work attempts to to side-step both these problems by limiting its scope to refinements of the published Torrey. Thus it contains only references to additional, or supplementary, information, published in the form of corrections, new discoveries, significant new biographical detail or deletions to Torrey's original work. Since these new discoveries and corrections tend to make their way into the periodical literature more frequently than elsewhere, this is predominantly an index to the major genealogical journals published since 1960 (as seen in the reference list). Several of the all-my-ancestry style books done since Torrey's death, most notably *The Ancestry of Abel Lunt*, by Walter Goodwin Davis, have made contributions and are included here. A significant number of new entries were spontaneously offered by some of the leading genealogical researchers in this area from their own unpublished work. Such entries are an advance look at what may be appearing in print in the years to come. Lastly, a few corrections, particularly in the form of deletions, are offered. There are many more discoveries of this type out there. I continue to keep a file of them and would be glad to have such items brought to my attention. Just received, but too late to include in this work, is *Fifty Great Migration Colonists To New England & Their Origins*, published by John Brooks Threlfall, (Madison, Wis., 1990), containing a number of new discoveries worthy of attention.

Arrangement

The presentation of these entries follows a simple format. Torrey originally used a fairly complex set of notations, such as "[ ]" to show a maiden name not found in a marriage record. After polling a number of readers at the New England Historic Genealogical Society who were frequent users of Torrey's work, and finding that they were happily oblivious of the meaning of most of his special notations, the notation system was dropped here.

Entries are arranged alphabetically by groom. An every-name index follows the main text.

The groom is presented first: last name in capitals, first name and a superscript indicating his generation from the immigrant if this information is provided in the source, followed by the years of his birth (or baptism, indicated by "bp") and death in parentheses. If these dates are approximate, they are preceded by a "c" as an abbreviation for "circa." The next element is the indicator of which marriage this is for the groom. If it is an only marriage, an "&" is used. If one of multiple marriages for the groom, a 1/wf, 2/wf, etc., appears.

The bride's name appears next: first name first, a superscript if her generation is indicated in the reference work, then her surname in capitals. If her maiden name is unknown, and it is her first marriage, her given name is followed by a blank: " _____." If she is a widow or divorced, her maiden name appears in parentheses, in the usual manner, the parentheses remaining empty if her maiden name is unknown. Other married names are presented in order, with all but the last in parentheses. If her subsequent or previous marriages or divorces are mentioned in the article being referenced, they are listed after her dates of birth and death.

The marriage date, if given, is the next element, followed by the place(s), either of the marriage or of primary residence. If no marriage date is known, but an early occurrence such as a child's birth, joint deed, or court appearance is mentioned, that year with "bef" for before or "aft" for after is shown.

Lastly, the reference for the entire item is entered in abbreviated form with volume and page number, if applicable.

A few additional abbreviations are used, e.g., "+" indicates that a person lived beyond the listed date; "m" is married; "w of Samuel" means widow of Samuel. State, or more properly, colony, designations are given only when it may be unclear whether the town in New England or England is meant.

Use

With the printed version of the original *New England Marriages Prior to 1700* (Genealogical Publishing Company, 1985), this Torrey supplement can be used in a variety of ways to develop clues for eighteenth- and nineteenth-century research, as well as identifying or eliminating seventeenth-century ancestors.

Although many of the entries here are drawn from articles concerned with the identification of a woman's maiden name, often from English records, a good percentage come from multi-generational studies, often running five or six generations, well into the eighteenth century. Thus, this indexes not only the seventeenth-century couple, but also leads the researcher to later generations of many families, too.

The appearance of certain given names can provide clues to possible ancestry. For instance, many unusual women's names tend to run in families. Names such as "Olive," "Jael," "Jerusha," "Violet," "Rooksby," and "Desire" are strongly identified with particular surnames, and can be indicative of the maiden name of a mother or grandmother when seen in later generations.

The geographical distribution of certain surnames can often provide clues for later work. Especially in the cases of very common surnames, such as Smith or Brown, the identification of the locality can do much to limit a search by way of process of elimination. Use of the locality listing at the end of each of these entries, combined with a knowledge of likely migration patterns, may determine the area of a later search.

Patterns in the New Discoveries

Significant new discoveries pertaining to seventeenth-century New England continue to appear at a fairly steady rate, just better than twenty per year. In part this is a function of the number of publications appearing each year and of the number of serious researchers using original documents. A significant proportion of the entries in this supplement derive from two relatively neglected areas of study: English marriages of colonial immigrants and marriages from the 1690s.

The former was neglected in Torrey's time, not so much from lack of trying, but because convenient indexes were not readily available. The International Genealogical Index has done much to make long-distance research easier, and a fair number of recent discoveries owe their success to its use as an index. The appearance of Peter Wilson Coldham's two volumes of seventeenth-century emigration records, *The Complete Book of Emigrants 1607-1660* (Genealogical Publishing Company, 1987) and *The Complete Book of Emigrants 1661-1699* (Genealogical Publishing Company, 1990), has been material in filling the information void for this type of research. In recent years, the great popularity of old classics in reprint form, such as Henry F. Waters' two-volume set, *Genealogical Gleanings in England* and Michael Ghirelli's *A List of Emigrants from England To America 1682-1692*, has made this early information much more accessible.

The 1690s suffered from a lack of interest. For descendants of immigrants of the Great Migration period, marriages in the 1690s belonged predominantly to the fourth generation, often beyond the scope of early three-generational studies.

Another factor which has had an effect on research surrounding the 1690s is the failure of many standard finding-aids to cover the period. More than a few of the indexing projects begun by the W.P.A. come to a stop in the late 1680s or early 1690s. Also, for several years during this decade, there was no requirement to record marriages in Massachusetts towns.

Two other neglected areas which are touched on in this supplement have to do with childless couples and families on Long Island.

Discoveries included here also surfaced through re-examination of a number of published versions of complicated court records, particularly abstracts of probate court material and of early Quarterly and Particular courts.

A very useful feature of the present index is that discoveries in the last thirty years were often made in the most unexpected places, especially in books and articles of an instructional or descriptive nature. Instead of the bald statements of fact so popular in Torrey's day, current writers sometimes treat us to a step-by-step explanation of how a find was made.

The techniques described are varied and often unique in approach. Rather than merely culling the data from such articles, we are able to gain an appreciation of what they teach, and this can be very helpful in future searches.

Several of the unpublished items submitted from the work of leading researchers are the results of techniques neglected since the era of the great town histories, when entire settlements were studied, rather than simply individual families. Most notable among these new efforts is *The Great Migration Study Project*, sponsored by the New England Historic Genealogical Society and conducted by Robert Charles Anderson, F.A.S.G. By looking at communities in their entirety, it is possible that missing links may be discovered or at least deduced with a reasonable degree of certainty. We may expect many new finds from this source.

Likewise, the study of immigrant clusters in their English home parishes has brought many breakthroughs in recent years, and is expected to continue to do so. An excellent example of this cluster phenomenon, highlighting several Lynn, Massachusetts, families, appeared in *The American Genealogist* in April 1990 (65:65-9).

A relatively small number of discoveries presented here were made through the re-examination of original records which had been misused or misread. It was not uncommon for many of the great genealogists of past generations to employ local researchers to make abstracts of records which were not easily available to the primary researcher. Through misreadings and lack of attention to detail, mistakes sometimes were made. For decades, the errors have been perpetuated, finally to be corrected by a closer look at the original record.

The journals indexed here, *The American Genealogist, The New England Historical and Genealogical Register, The National Genealogical Society Quarterly, The New York Genealogical and Biographical Record, The Mayflower Descendant,* and *The Genealogist,* are the premier forums for New England discoveries. Many future finds can be expected to surface in their pages in the same reliable manner in which they appeared in Torrey's time.

REFERENCES

Abel Lunt   Walter Goodwin Davis, *The Ancestry of Abel Lunt,*
1769-1806 of Newbury, Massachusetts (Portland, ME:
The Anthoensen Press, 1963)

AMacE   The unpublished research of Andrew B.W.
MacEwen, P.O. Box 97, Stockton Springs, ME 04981

ASBO   Dean Crawford Smith, *The Ancestry of Samuel*
Blanchard Ordway (Boston: New England Historic
Genealogical Society, 1990)

DCD   The unpublished research of David Curtis Dearborn,
Reference Librarian, New England Historic
Genealogical Society, 101 Newbury Street, Boston,
MA 02116

EIHC   *Essex Institute Historical Collections,* Essex
Institute, Salem, MA

Essex Probate   Original probate records at the Registry of
Probate for Essex County, Salem, MA

EQC   *Records and Files of the Quarterly Courts of Essex*
County, Massachusetts. 9 vols. (Salem, MA: Essex
Institute, 1911-1975)

Fiske   Jane Fletcher Fiske, *Thomas Cooke of Rhode Island.*
2 vols. (Boxford, MA, 1987)

Gen.Adv.   *The Genealogical Advertiser, A Quarterly Magazine*
of Family History, Lucy Hall Greenlaw, ed., 4 vols.
1898-1901. (Reprint 4 vols. in 1. Baltimore:
Genealogical Publishing Co., 1974)

GFS   The unpublished research of George Freeman
Sanborn Jr., Director of Library Operations, New
England Historic Genealogical Society, 101
Newbury Street, Boston, MA 02116

HQ	*Heritage Quest: The International Genealogy Forum,* Orting, WA 98360
LB	Lost Babes, manuscript in preparation; containing abstracts from the Essex County General Sessions records, compiled by Melinde Lutz Sanborn
LCVR	Benjamin Franklin Wilbour, *Little Compton Families, From Records Compiled by Benjamin Franklin Wilbour* (Little Compton, RI: Little Compton Historical Society, 1967)
LND	Sybil Noyes, Charles Thornton Libby, and Walter Goodwin Davis, *The Genealogical Dictionary of Maine and New Hampshire.* 5 parts. 1928-1939. (Reprint 5 parts in 1. Baltimore: Genealogical Publishing Company, 1972)
MD	*The Mayflower Descendant,* 101 Newbury Street, Boston, MA 02116
NGSQ	*The National Genealogical Society Quarterly,* 4527 Seventeenth Street North, Arlington, VA 22207-2399
NYGBR	*The New York Genealogical and Biographical Record,* 122 East 58th Street, New York, NY 10022
PCRG	Plymouth Colony Research Group, unpublished research offered by Ruth Wilder Sherman, 128 Massasoit Drive, Warwick, RI 02888
PCR	*Records of the Colony of New Plymouth in New England,* Nathaniel B. Shurtless and David Pulsifer, eds. 12 vols. (Boston: Commonwealth of Massachusetts, 1855-1861)
Pynchon Court Book	*Colonial Justice in Western Massachusetts,* Joseph H. Smith, ed. (Cambridge: Harvard University Press, 1961)

RCA	The unpublished research of Robert Charles Anderson, 5069 Cottonwood Lane, Salt Lake City, UT 84117
RI Friends records per PCRG	From the Rhode Island Friends records, available on microfilm at the Rhode Island Historical Society, Providence, RI, pointed out by the Plymouth Colony Research Group
Smith	Frederick Kinsman Smith, *The Family of Richard Smith of Smithtown, L.I.* (Smithtown, 1967)
Suffolk Deed	Original deeds at the Registry of Deeds for Suffolk County at Boston, MA
Swansea Book A	Original Swansea, Massachusetts town records
TAG	*The American Genealogist*, 128 Massasoit Drive, Warwick, RI 02888
TG	*The Genealogist*, 255 North 200 West, Salt Lake City, UT 84103-4545
VR per PCRG	From vital records of the indicated towns pointed out by the Plymouth Colony Research Group

SUPPLEMENT TO TORREY'S

NEW ENGLAND MARRIAGES PRIOR TO 1700

ABELL, James & Sarah **BOWEN**; m 1686 Rehoboth [VR per PCRG]

ADAMS, Abraham (c1639-1714) & Mary **PETTINGILL** (1652-1705); m 16 Nov 1670 Newbury [Abel Lunt, p.53]

ADAMS, George[1] (-1696) & Frances **TAYLOR** (-1696+); m bef 1645, Watertown [TAG 55:207]

ADAMS, Jonathan[2] (c1643-1707) & Rebecca **ANDREWS** (c1655-1731); m c1671 Falmouth [TG 3:62]

ADDIS, William[1] & Millicent **WOOD**; m bef 1623 Harescomb, Eng/New London [TAG 58:215; 57:181]

ALBEE, John (-1675) & Jane **HOLBROOK**; m2 Alexander **BALCOM**; m 18 Oct 1671 Medfield/Mendon [TAG 48:122]

ALBERTSON, Derrick[1] & Willmet ____; Oyster Bay [NYGBR 109:205]

ALBERTSON, Derrick[2] & Dinah **COLES**; m bef 10 Nov 1692 Oyster Bay [NYGBR 109:206]

ALCOCK, Philip (c1648-1715) & 2/wf Sarah (**GREEN**) **BUTLER** (1642-), w of Nathaniel; m 4 Apr 1699 New Haven/Wethersfield [TAG 46:10]

ALLEN, James[3] (c1678-1723/4) & Mary **BOURNE** (1678-1722); m c1700 Chilmark [REG 118:204]

ALLEN, John & Elizabeth **BACON**; m 1650 [RI Friends records per PCRG]

ALLEN, John[4] & Rebecca ____, m2 Joseph[2] **LANDERS** [REG 124:45]

ALLEN, Joshua & Mary ?CROWELL (-1727) m2 William MORE; m bef 1682 [REG 125:232-4]

ALLEN, Richard (1673-1730/1) & Hannah BUTLER (c1673-); m c1695 Sandwich [REG 127:24]

ALLERTON, Isaac[1] (-1659) & 3/wf Joanna SWINNERTON; m bet 1634-1644, Plymouth [REG 124:133 & TAG 60:159]

ALVORD, Benedict & Joan NEWTON (bp 1616/7-), sister of Anthony; m 1640 Watertown [TAG 65:14-16]

ANDREWS, James[2] (1625/6-1704) & 1/wf Dorcas[2] MITTON (c1627-1695/6); m c1645-6, Portland [TG 3:59]

ANNIS, Abraham[2] (1668-bef 1751) & Hannah ?BADGER (1673-by 1724); m c1692 Newbury [ASBO, p.127]

ANNIS, Anthony & Jane RUNDLETT, delete - error for John ANTHONY [LND p.66]

ANNIS, Isaac[2] (c1673-by 1712) & Rebecca[4] BAILEY (1675-1748); m2 Shimuel GRIFFIN; m by 1700 Newbury [ASBO, p.124]

ASLEBEE, John (c1614-1671) & Rebecca AYER (-bef 1702); m2 George KEYSER, 8 Oct 1648 Newbury [TAG 40:231]

ATWOOD, Nathaniel[2] (c1650/1-1724) & Mary LUCAS (1659/60-1736); m bef 1684 Plymouth [TAG 41:202]

AYER, Joseph (1658/9-1698+) & Sarah[2] CORLISS (1663/4-1698+); m 24 Nov 1686 Haverhill [ASBO, p.212]

AYER, Zachariah[3] (1657-1696+) & Elizabeth[2] CHASE (1657-1696+); did not m2 Daniel FAVOR; m 27 June 1678 Andover [ASBO, p.175]

BADLAM, William[1] (c1660s-bef 1718) & 1/wf Joane _____ (c1660-c1687-90); m bef 1684, Boston/Weymouth [REG 141:3]

BADLAM, William[1] (1660s-bef 1718) & 2/wf Mary FRENCH (1662-bef 1718); m c1690 Weymouth/Boston [REG 141:3]

BAGLEY, Orlando[2] (1658-c1728/9) & 1/wf Sarah SARGENT (1651/2-1701); m 22 Dec 1681 Amesbury [ASBO, p.124]

BAILEY, John & Ann BOURNE, m2 Thomas TRANTOR; m 9 May 1677 Marshfield [TAG 40:33-4]

BAKER, Samuel (c1665-) & Sarah SNOW (1680-); m 27 Feb 1699 Marshfield [REG 124:119]

BAKER, William (c1655-1743) & 1/wf Sarah FITTS (1661-bef 1722); m 30 Dec 1689 Ipswich [ASBO, p.89]

BALCOM, Alexander[1] & Jane (HOLBROOK) ALBEE, w of John; m c1676 Providence [TAG 48:122]

BALLINE, Samuel & Experience SABIN; m 1672 Rehoboth [VR per PCRG]

BANGS, Jonathan (1640-1728) & 1/wf Mary MAYO (-1711); m 16 Jul 1664 Eastham [TAG 60:159 & MD 4:29]

BARBER, Thomas (c1645-1690+) & Anne[2] CHASE (1647-1690+); m 27 Apr 1671 Newbury/Suffield [ASBO, p.172]

BARNUM, Thomas & Sarah (THOMPSON) HURD (-1717/8), w of John [TAG 50:3]

BARTRUM, William & Sarah ____; m bef 1688 Swansey [Gen. Adv. 4:58]

BATE, Edward[1] (bp 1606-1686) & Susanna PUTNAM (bp 1609/10-); m 26 Jan 1631/2 Drayton Beauchamp, co Bucks/Weymouth [TAG 65:94]

BASSETT, Nathaniel[2] (c1628-1709/10) & Dorcas JOYCE (not Mary) (c1640-1707); m c1661 Yarmouth/Chatham [TAG 43:3]

BATH, William & Eleanor ( ) ELLENWOOD (c1636-), w of Ralph; m bef June 1677 Beverly [EQC 4:216; 6:288]

BEACKINTON, ____ & Ann PEDERICK?; m bef 1693, Marblehead [LB]

BENNETT, William[1] (c1620-1682) & Jane ____ (c1622-1693); m bef 1643 East Budleigh, co Devon/Manchester, MA [ASBO, p.139]

BENSON, Isaac[3] & Mary[3] BUMPUS (bp 1671-); m 17 Mar 1698/9 Scituate [TAG 43:69]

BENSON, John[1] (c1608-1678) & Mary WILLIAMS (c1610-1681); m 14 Oct 1633 Caversham, Eng/Hull [REG 142:269]

BENSON, John[2] (c1635-1711) & Elizabeth MARSH (1646-1704); m c1664, Hull [REG 142:270]

BETTYS, ____ & Miriam[2] TYLER (c1655-8-), dau of John; m aft 1697 Portsmouth, RI [TAG 52:221]

BIAM, Abraham & Experience ALVORD; m 1672 Scituate [VR per PCRG]

BIDFORD, Samuel & Sarah JOANS; m 18 Nov 1697 Harwich [TAG 60:158]

BILL, James[1] & 1/wf Anne ?TUTTLE (-bef 1627); m bef 11 Sep 1613 Ringstead, Notts [TAG 60:200]

BILL, James[1] & 2/wf Dorothy _____ (-1640+); m bef Mar 1626/7 Boston [TAG 60:200]

BIRCHARD, Thomas[1] (bp 1595-by 1684) & 1/wf Mary ROBINSON (1596-1655); m 23 Oct 1620 Fairstead, co. Essex/Roxbury [TAG 51:18]

BIRCHARD, Thomas[1] (bp 1595-by 1684) & 2/wf Katherine ( ) ANDREWS; Roxbury [TAG 51:18]

BIRCHARD, Thomas[1] (bp 1595-by 1684) & 3/wf Deobrah _____ (-1680); Roxbury [TAG 51:18]

BISHOP, Edward (not Edward[1]) & Bridget (PLAYFER)(WASSILBE) OLIVER (-1692) w of Thomas; m bef 1680 Salem [TAG 57:129-38, 64:207]

BLAISDELL, John[3] (1668-1733) & Elizabeth[2] (CHALLIS) HOYT (bef 1671-1744+); m 6 Jan 1692/3 Amesbury [ASBO, p.151]

BLAND, John (alias SMITH) (-1667) & 1/wf Isabel DRAKE (-1639); m bef 1613 Eng [TAG 61:22]

BLANEY, John[2] (1661-1726) & Elizabeth PURCHASE (not WILLIAMS) (c1645-1726+); m 20 Dec 1683 Marblehead [TG 3:54]

BLINMAN, Richard (-1687) & Mary ?PARKE, m bef 1642 Gloucester/New London [TG 4:182]

BLINN, James[2] (c1673-1731) & Margaret DENNISON (1677-1736); m 6 Dec 1698 Boston [REG 143:310]

BLINN, Peter[2] & Hannah ?CRAMPTON; m bef 7 Mar 1696/7 Guilford [REG 143:308]

BLISS, Thomas (-1650/1) & 1/wf Margaret HULINS (c1595-1684); m 18 Oct 1621 St. Nicholas, co Gloucester/Hartford, CT [TAG 52:193; 60:202]

BLOSSOM, Thomas[1] & Anne HELSDON, m2 Henry ROWLEY; m 10 Nov 1605 Cambridge, Eng/Plymouth [TAG 63:74]

BLOWER, John[1] (-1675) & Tabitha _____; m bef 1654/5 Barnstable/ Boston [TAG 52:74]

BOOTH, George & Elizabeth WILKINS; m bef 30 Dec 1692 Salem [REG 144:54]

BORDEN, John[1] (-1636) & Joan ___ (-1691), m2 bef 1638 John GAY; m Eng bef 1630/Dedham [REG 130:39]

BOTSFORD, Samuel[3] (1670-1745) & Hannah (not widow SMITH) (- 1732); m bef 1700 Milford [TAG 59:196]

BOUENTON, Thomas, see BUFFINGTON

BOURNE, Shearjashub (c1643-1718/19) & Bathsheba SKIFFE (1648-1714); m c1673 Sandwich [REG 118:203]

BOURNE, Timothy[3] (1666-1744) & Temperance SWIFT (c1668-1746); m c1688 Sandwich [REG 118:205]

BOWDITCH, William (-1681) & Sarah BEARE (-1699+); m 15 Sep 1663 Thornecombe, co Devon/Salem [NGSQ 69:278]

BOWEN, Griffith[1] & Margaret FLEMING (only wife); m 1627 Wales/Boston/Swanzey [NGSQ 67:163]

BOWEN, Thomas & Elizabeth NICHOLS; m2 Samuel FULLER; m bef 1663 [MD 39:86]

BOWERMAN, Thomas[2] (1648-) & Mary[2] HARPER (1655-); m 7 4mo 1678 Sandwich [TAG 48:217]

BRACKETT, Peter (1608-) & 1/wf Martha RAY; m 4 Oct 1632 Cavendish, Eng [TAG 52:73]

BRACKETT, Peter[1] (1608-) & 2/wf Priscilla _____ [TAG 52:73]

BRACKETT, Peter[1] (1608-) & 3/wf Mary ( ) WILLIAMS, w of Nathaniel, Boston [TAG 52:73]

BRACKETT, Richard (1611-1691) & Alice BLOWER (bp 1615-1690); m 16 Jan 1633/4 St. Katherine by the Tower, London/ Boston [TAG 52:65; 56:99; REG 127:17]

BRADSHAW, Humprhey & Martha (DAVIES) RUSSELL (-1695), w of William, m3 Thomas HALL [TAG 44:83]

BRADSTREET, Dudley (1648-1706) & Anne **WOOD** (not **WHITE**) **PRICE**, w of Theodore; m 12 Nov 1673 Salem [REG 139:139]

BREWSTER, Nathaniel & 2/wf Sarah **LUDLOW** (c1643-   ); m after Feb 1660 Dublin, Ire/Boston/Setauket [NGSQ 51:234]

BREWSTER, William (?1557-1644) & Mary **STUBBE**? (-1627); m bef 1593 Eng [REG 128:288]

BRIGGS, Hugh^2 (-1692+) & Martha^2 **EVERSON** (-1736/7); m 1 Mar 1682/3 Taunton/Plympton [REG 125:82]

BRIGGS, John^1 (bp 1595-   ) & Agnes **THAYER** (bp 1607-   ); m 11 Nov 1633 Thornbury, Gloucestershire/Taunton, MA [TAG 59:179]

BRIGGS, John^3 (1672-1750) & 1/wf Hannah **HOLLOWAY** (-bef 1727); m bef 1699 Norton/Taunton [REG 125:84]

BRIGGS, John^3 (1672-1750) & 2/wf Mary **BURT** (-c1733); m 29 May 1727 Taunton/Norton [REG 125:84]

BRIGGS, Samuel^2 (-1675+) & Elizabeth **ELLIS** (c1645-1675+); m c1664 Sandwich [REG 119:172]

BRIGGS, William^2 (c1649-1728) & 1/wf Sarah **MACOMBER** (c1643-1680); m 6 Nov 1666 Dorchester/Marshfield [REG 125:82]

BRIGGS, William^2 (c1649-1728) & 2/wf ?Abigail **MASON**; m 2 Jul 1680 Dedham [REG 125:82]

BRIMBLECOM, John^1 (bp 1622-1678) & Tabitha _____ (only wife); m c1640 Modbury, co Devon/Marblehead [DCD]

BRIMBLECOM, John (-1656+) & Barbara (   ) **DAVIS**, w of George, m3 Thomas **CHADWELL**; m 14 Jan 1655 Lynn/Boston [DCD]

BROCK, Henry & Elizabeth **ALDOUS** (bp 1593/4-   ); m c1619 Dedham [REG 144:130]

BROCK, Peter (-1707) & Sarah _____ (c1677-1717), m2 Henry **BEERE**/ **BEERS**; m c1696 Newport [TAG 65:195]

BRONSON, John (1602-1680) & Frances **HILLS** (-1680+); m 19 Nov 1626 Halstead, co Essex/Farmington, CT [TAG 38:199]

BRONSON, Richard (-1687) & 2/wf _____ _____ (-c1665); m c1646/7 Farmington [TAG 38:206]

BRONSON, Richard (-1687) & 3/wf Elizabeth ( ) CARPENTER ORVIS, w of David, w of George; m c1666 Farmington, CT [TAG 38:206]

BROOKS, Richard & Mary (BLANCHARD) COOPER (c1645-60-bef 1729), w of Josiah [REG 140:315]

BROWN, Abraham (1649-1733) & Elizabeth[2] SHEPARD (c1655-1733+); m 15 June 1675 Salisbury [ASBO, p.373]

BROWN, Boaz (1641/2-1724) & 1/wf Mary WINSHIP (1641-bef 1695); m 8 Nov 1664 Concord [REG 140:317]

BROWN, Boaz (1641/2-1724, not Jr.) & 2/wf Mary (FULLER) RICHARDS, (-1715) w of John; m 30 Sep 1695 Stow/Dedham [REG 140:317]

BROWN, Robert & Sarah HARKER; m bef 1680s Boston [Suffolk Deed 12:282]

BROWN, Thomas (1667-1739) & Rachel POULTER (1670/1-1710+); m c1690 Lexington [REG 141:221]

BRUCE, Roger[2] (c1670-1733) & Elizabeth FORBUSH (1669-by 1746); m c1690 Sudbury/Marlborough [REG 136:301]

BRUCE, Thomas[1] (-c1714-21) & Magdalen _____ (-c1706-9); m bef 1665 Sudbury/Marlborough [REG 136:296]

BUCK, Emanuel[1] (1621-1705-7) & 2/wf Mary ARNOLD (-bef 1664); m 17 Apr 1658 Wethersfield [TAG 44:169]

BUFFINGTON, Benjamin[2] (1675-bef 1739) & Hannah SOUTHWICK (1677-1735+); m bef 1699 Salem/Swansea [TAG 62:182]

BUFFINGTON, Thomas (1644-bef 28 Aug 1729) & Sarah SOUTHWICK (1644-1733+); Salem/Swansea [TAG 62:184]

BUMPAS, John (1636-1715/6)& Sarah _____ (-1710+); m bef 1670 Scituate/ Middleboro/Rochester [TAG 43:69]

BURKE, Richard (1671-) & Abigail SAWTELL (1671/2-1716); m bef 1691 Sudbury [REG 126:6]

BURMAN, Thomas & Hannah _____; m bef 1663 Barnstable [MD 18:63]

BURROUGHS, George (?1650-1692) & 3/wf Mary _____ (-1712+); m2 Michael HOMER, m3 Christopher HALL; m c1690 Salem [TAG 56:43]

BURROUGHS, Jeremiah & _____ HEWES, m2 John MENDALL [TAG 40:33]

BURSLEY, Thomas & Joanna _____; m bef 1660 [PCR 3:201]

BUSCOTE, Peter[1] & Mary MAY; m 20 Nov 1631 Hartland, co Devon/ Warwick, RI [TAG 58:230]

BUTLER, Daniel[2] (c1642-bef 1717) & Elizabeth HOUSE (-1689-1717); m 8 2mo 1665 Sandwich [REG 127:22]

BUTLER, Nathaniel (1641-1697/8) & Sarah GREEN (1642-); m2 Philip ALCOCK; m bef 1668 Wethersfield [TAG 46:10]

BUTLER, Samuel (1640-) & Elizabeth _____ (-1681); m bef 1665 Haddam, CT [TAG 60:29]

BUTTOLPH, George[3] (1667-1696) & Elizabeth probably BUCK, (1670-1752); m2 Robert LATIMER; m bef 1690 Wethersfield [TAG 58:138]

BUTTOLPH, John (-1693) & Abigail (FITCH) MASON (1650-); w of John[2]; m 1682 Norwich [TAG 40:54]

BUTTOLPH, John[2] (-1692/3) & 3/wf Susanna (CLARK)(KELLY) SANFORD; w of James, w of Nathaniel; m bef 1687 Wethersfield [TAG 58:136]

CALLUM, Caleb Sr. (-by 1692/3) & Elizabeth DYNN (-1716), m2 Richard COMER/COMAN; m c1680 Salem, MA [DCD]

CALLUM, John & Elizabeth BEANS (she did not m2 Richard COMER/COMAN; m 30 Nov 1685 Salem [DCD]

CANFIELD, Nathaniel & Sarah WILLOUGHBY; m bef 12 May 1662 Eng/Norwalk [REG 118:296]

CANFIELD, Samuel & Elizabeth MERWIN (not WILLOUGHBY) (bef 1650-1697+); m bef 1697 Norwich [REG 118:296]

CARGILL, David (c1661-1734) & Janet SMITH (c1664-1745); m c1680 Derry, No. Ireland/Londonderry, NH [REG 117:244]

CARPENTER, David & Elizabeth _____; m2 George ORVIS; m3 Richard BRONSON [TAG 38:206]

CARR, Caleb & Phillipa GREEN (1658-by 1706), m2 Charles DICKINSON [TAG 42:189]

CASE, Henry (1659-1740) & Tabitha VAIL (-1735) Southold, LI [TAG 38:183]

CASWELL, Thomas[2] (1650\1-1725-6) & 2/wf Mary RAMSDEN; m 2 Dec 1691 Taunton [MD 39:69]

CAZNEAU, Paix (-1720) & Margaret GERMAINE (1671-1769); m bef 1696 Boston/Roxbury/Wrentham [REG 142:127]

CHADBOURNE, William[1] (bp 1582-1643+) & Elizabeth SPARRY; m 8 Oct 1609 Tamworth, co Stafford/Portsmouth [GFS]

CHADWELL, Thomas & 2/wf Barbara (   ) (DAVIS BRIMBLECOM, w of George, w of John; m aft 1656 Lynn/Boston [DCD]

CHALLIS, John[2] (c1677-1742) & Sarah[2] FRAME (c1680-1751+); m 26 Jan 1698/9 Salisbury [ASBO, p.153]

CHALLIS, Thomas[2] (1673-c1752) & 1/wf Mary[3] COLBY (c1669-bef 1727); m bef 3 Sep 1696 Amesbury [TAG 49:172; ASBO, p.154]

CHALLIS, William[2] (1663-by 1726) & Margaret[3] FOWLER (1673-1726+); m 2 Jan 1698/9 Salisbury [ASBO, p.152]

CHAMBERLAIN, Francis & perhaps Agnes HAIDEN; m 1613/4 Ugley, co Essex [TAG 51:151]

CHAMBERLAIN, Thomas & Mary (?POPE)(POULTER) PARKER (c1596-1692/3), w of John[1], w of John [REG 141:217]

CHAPMAN, Edward & Elizabeth SHERWIN; m bef 31 Mar 1696 [REG 144:54]

CHAPPELL, John & Elizabeth (CARPENTER) JONES (1644-1694+), w of Richard; m3 _____ HILL [TAG 41:42]

CHASE, Aquila[2] (1652-1720) & Esther BOND (1655-1722/3+); m c1673 Newbury [ASBO, p.174]

CHASE, Daniel[2] (1661-1706/7) & Martha[3] KIMBALL (1664-1713+); m 25 Aug 1683 Newbury [ASBO, p.175]

CHASE, John[2] (1655-1739/40) & 1/wf Elizabeth[2] BINGLEY (1660-bef 1687); m 23 May 1677 Newbury [ASBO, p.175]

CHASE, John[2] (1655-1739/40) & 2/wf Lydia[2] CHALLIS (1665-1736+); m 21 Dec 1687 Salisbury [ASBO, p.175]

CHASE, Thomas[2] (1654-1732-4) & 1/wf Rebecca[2] FOLLANSBEE (c1658-1711); m 22 Nov 1677 Newbury [ASBO, p.174]

CHENEY, Peter, Jr. & Mary (   ) HOLMES, w of Samuel[1] [ASBO, p.341]

CHILD, Ephraim[1] (c1593-1663) & Elizabeth (BOND) PALMER, w of Samuel; m 1624/5 Nayland, co Suffolk/Watertown [TAG 62:29]

CHILD, Shubael (1665-   ) & Abigail SANDERSON (-1693); m 27 Oct 1687 Watertown [REG 127:182]

CHILDS, Joseph & Elizabeth TROUANT; m bef 11 Apr 1696 Marshfield [TAG 40:33]

CHURCH, Caleb (c1646-bef 1722) & 3/wf Rebecca (   ) SCOTTOW, w of John; m 6 Nov 1691 Watertown [TAG 60:135]

CHURCHILL, John (-1723) & 1/wf Rebecca DELANO (-1709); m 28 Dec 1686 Plymouth [TAG 60:139; MD 13:204]

CLARK, Christopher & Rebecca EIRE; m c1647 Watertown [TAG 65:21]

CLARK, John (-1726/7) & Sarah[2] SMITH (1660-c1731); m bef 1683 Beverly [TAG 43:23]

CLARKE, William (c1608-1682/3) & Mary SHERMAN (-1693); m c1640 Lynn [TAG 39:101]

CLEEVE, George[1] & 1/wf Alice ABROOK; m 17 Oct 1612 London/Portland [REG 140:180]

CLEEVE, George[1] & 2/wf Alice SHORTOLL/STANSTALL?; m 22 Sep 1614 St Peter's Cornhill, London [REG 140:181]

CLEEVE, George[1] & 3/wf Frances OLNEY (-bef 1618); m c1615 London [REG 140:181]

CLEEVE, George[1] & 4/wf Joan PRICE; m 7 Sep 1618 Shrewsbury/Portland [REG 140:181]

CLIFTON, Savery (c1665-1753+) & Dorothy BURGES (1670-1725-7); m by 1690 Rochester [NGSQ 59:168]

COBB, John & Susannah BRIGGS; m bef 1696 Providence [NGSQ 73:25]

COGSWELL, Adam[3] (1666/7-1749) & Abigail WISE (1666-   ); m c1687 Ipswich [TAG 56:82; 60:159]

COLBY, James & _____ _____; m bef 1679 Rehoboth [PCR 6:8, 13]

COLCORD, Edward[1] (c1615-1681/2) & Anne WARD (c1622-1688/9); m c1640 Hampton [REG 141:120]

COLDHAM, Thomas[1] (-1675) & Joanna _____ (-1687); m bef 1623 Eng/Lynn [REG 125:24]

COLE, James & Ann ?WALLINGTON (-1679/80); m 6 Dec 1625 St Dunstan's Stepney/Hartford, CT [TAG 40:74]

COLE, James[3] (1655-) & Mary[2] CADMAN?; m bef 1696 Swanzey [TAG 64:140]

COLEMAN, Thomas & Margaret MUSHIT; m 10 Dec 1679 Marshfield [TAG 60:159]

COMER/COMAN, Richard & Martha GILBERT; m 23 Oct 1663 Salem [DCD]

COMER/COMAN, Richard[2] (-1716) & 1/wf Martha REWE; m 25 Oct 1683 Salem [DCD]

COMER/COMAN, Richard[2] (-1716) & 2/wf Elizabeth (DYNN) CALLUM, w of Caleb Sr.; m 4 Feb 1692/3 Salem/Providence [DCD]

COOK, George[2] (c1647-1711+) & Ann _____ (-1689+); m bef 1683 Long Island [Fiske 1:40]

COOKE, John[2] (-1704/5) & Phebe WEEDEN (-1734+); m2 William PECKHAM; m c1676 Warwick div 1684 [TAG 52:5; 60:159]

COOKE, John & 2/wf Hannah HARRIS; m c1690 Providence/Middletown [TAG 52:6]

COOK, John[3] (c1652-1727) & Mary HAVENS? (c1656-1754); m bef 1675 Tiverton [Fiske 1:47]

COOK, John[3] (1656-1737) & Ruth SHAW (1660-1737+); m c1680 Portsmouth, RI/Tiverton [Fiske 1:63]

COOKE, Thomas[1] (bp 1600-1677) & 1/wf Mary _____ (-by 1673) Taunton [Fiske 1:13]

COOKE, Thomas[1] (bp1600-1677) & 2/wf Mary ?SHEARMAN (1645-) not SLOCUM, m2 Jeremiah BROWN c1679; Kingstown [Fiske 1:13]

COOKE, Walter (-1695/6) & Catherine **BRENTON** (-1695/6); m bef 1674 Mendon [REG 128:154]

COOLIDGE, John[1] (bp 1604-1691) & Mary[1] **RAVENS** (bp 1602-1691); m c1628 Eng/Watertown [TAG 62:164]

COOMBS, John (1664-1709/10) & Elizabeth **(BALLENTINE)** **(GREENLAND) YELLINGS** (1659-   ); w of David; w of Roger; m c1687/8 Boston [TAG 46:130]

COOPER, John & Wilbroe **(GRIGGS) PIERSON**, w of William; m 1618 Olney, Eng [TAG 64:196]

COOPER, Josiah (-1678) & 2/wf Mary **BLANCHARD** (c1645-50-bef 1729); m2 Richard **BROOKS**; m bef 1676 Boston [REG 140:315]

COPP, Aaron[3] (c1675-bef 1730) & Mary[3] **HEATH** (1672-1730+); m 30 Dec 1698 Haverhill [ASBO, p.316]

CORLISS, George[1] (c1617-1686) & Joanna **DAVIS** (c1624-1690s); m2 James[1] Ordway; m 26 Oct 1645 Haverhill [ASBO, p.207]

CORLISS, John[2] (1647/8-1697/8) & 1/wf Mary[2] **WILFORD** (1667-   ); m2 William[2] **WHITTAKER**; m 17 Dec 1684 Haverhill [ASBO, p.213]

CORNELL, Samuel[2] & Grissell **(STRANGE) FISH** (c1650-   ) w of Thomas[2]; m c1686 Dartmouth [TAG 54:25]

CORNELL, Thomas[2] (1627-1673) & 1/wf Elizabeth _____ (not **FISCOCK**); m bef 1657 Portsmouth [TAG 58:78]

CORNWELL, William (-1678) & 1/wf Joan **RANKE**; m 27 Sep 1632 Fairsted, co Essex [TAG 51:115]

COTTRELL, Nicholas (not Jabez) (-c1711) & Anna **PEABODY** (-bef 1711); m bef 22 Mar 1686/7 Stonington/Newport [REG 117:97]

CRISPE, Eleazar (1641/2-1726+) & Elizabeth _____; m bef 1700 Groton [TAG 62:27]

CRITTENDEN, Abraham Jr. (-1694) & Susanna **GREGSON** (c1637-1712); m 13 May 1661 New Haven [REG 128:73]

CROCKER, Francis & Mary **GAUNT** (-1693?); lic. 2 Mar 1646/7 Barnstable/Scituate [TAG 60:159]

CROSS, Robert[1] (c1613-bef 1702) & 1/wf Anna[2] JORDAN (c1615-1677); m 20 Aug 1635 Ipswich [ASBO, p.223]

CROSS, Robert[1] (c1613-bef 1702) & 2/wf Mary _____ (c1653-1695+); m bet 1677-1680 Ipswich [ASBO, p.223]

CROSS, Thomas[3] (1667-by 1698) & Esther _____ (c1670-1702+); m c1690 Ipswich [ASBO, p.237]

CROWELL, Christopher[1] (c1629-1688) & 1/wf Deliverance[2] BENNETT (bp 1643-1680); m 8 Oct 1657 Salem [ASBO, p.249]

CROWELL, Christopher[1] (c1629-1688) & 2/wf Margaret _____ (-1695+); m bef 1688 Boston [ASBO, p.249]

CURTIS, Henry & Mary TAINTOR; m bef 1642 Watertown/Sudbury [TAG 65:22-3]

CURTIS, William[2] (1662-) & 2/wf Lydia HILL; m bef 4 Feb 1698/9 Salem [TAG 59:75]

CUTLER, Samuel (1661-1773!) & Sarah SAWTELL (1673/4-1731+); m 20 Jan 1691/2 Salem [REG 126:6]

CUTTING, Richard & Susanna _____ (-1684), m2 Henry KIMBALL, m3 Thomas LOW [TAG 55:26]

DALTON, Timothy & Ruth LEET; m 13 June 1615 Gislingham, co Suffolk [TAG 52:113]

DAVENPORT, Rev. John (1597-1670) & 1/wf Elizabeth _____ not (WOLLEY) (1603-1676); m bef 1635 Boston [TAG 52:216]

DAVENPORT, William[2] (c1665-1742) & 1/wf Elizabeth NICHOLS? (c1670-1697); m c1690s Hartford [TAG 43:86]

DAVIS, George (-1655) & Barbara _____, m2 John BRIMBLECOM, m3 Thomas CHADWELL; m bef 1647 Boston [DCD]

DAVOL, Jonathan Jr. (-1709) & Mary _____ (not Hannah); Dartmouth [TAG 65:148]

DAVOL, Joseph (not Benjamin) & Elizabeth PEABODY; m bef 1686 [REG 117:97]

DAVOL, Joseph & Mary SOULE (1679+-); m bef 1700 Dartmouth [TAG 38:165]

DAYTON, Caleb (1659-   ) & Hannah SAYRE?; m c1680-1 Southampton, LI [TAG 38:228]

DEANE, Walter (bp 1612-1693+) & Eleanor STRONG (c1613-1693+); m bef 1638 Taunton [TAG 59:227]

DENASHA, Thomas & Agnes CROCKER; m 16 Mar 1698/9 Boston [REG 132:38]

DENTON, Nathaniel[2] (bp 1629-1690) & Sarah ____; m by 1653 Long Island [NYGBR 120:12]

DENTON, Samuel[2] (bp 1631-by 1713/4) & Mary SMITH; m c1664 Hempstead [NYGBR 120:14]

DESBOROW, Samuel (c1615-1690) & Rose (HOBSON) PENNOYER (c1616-1698); w of Samuel; m aft 1654 Guilford [NGSQ 60:248]

DEXTER, Stephen (1657-1730) & Anna[3] SANDERS (c1673-1729/30+); m 27 Apr 1696 Barnstable [REG 127:252]

DICKINSON, Charles (-1740) & 2/wf Phillipa (GREENE) CARR (1658-by 1706); w of Caleb; m bef 1693 So. Kingstown, RI [TAG 42:189]

DICKSEY, John & Elizabeth ALLEN; m 1668 Swansey [Swansey Book A, p.93]

DIVEN, John & Hester ____; m by 1647 Lynn [Essex Probate #7719]

DOTEY, Joseph[2] (1651-c1732) & Deborah[2] ELLIS (c1652-1711); m c1673/4 Rochester [REG 119:173]

DOW, Joseph[3] (1663-1734/5) & 1/wf Mary[2] CHALLIS (1668-1697); m 25 May 1687 Salisbury [ASBO, p.152]

DOW, Stephen[2] & Joanna[2] (CORLISS) HUTCHINS (1650-1734), w of Joseph[2] [ASBO, p.210]

DOW, Thomas[2] (1653-1728) & 2/wf Susanna HILL (-1724); m by 1685 [TAG 60:75]

DUDLEY, Samuel[2] (1608-1683) & 3/wf Elizabeth (?SMITH) GILMAN; dau of Richard; w of Edward[2]; m c1655 Cambridge/Salisbury/Exeter [AMacE]

DUNHAM, Nathaniel[3] (c1662-   ) & 1/wf Mary TILSON (-1714); m 21 Jan 1691/2 Plymouth [TAG 62:7]

DURKEE, William[1] (c1634-1712) & Martha[2] CROSS (1643-1726/7); m 20 Dec 1664 Ipswich [ASBO, p.230]

DURRELL, Philip[1] (-1749) & _____ ?PURINGTON (-killed 1726); m bef 1685 Kennebunkport [REG 132:117]

EDDY, _____ & Edith BROWNSON (1655-); m bef 27 Feb 1684/5 Farmington [TAG 38:208]

EDWARDS, William[1] (bp 1618-c1680) & Agnes[1] (HARRIS) SPENCER (bp 1604-1680+); w of William; m 11 Dec 1645 Hartford [TAG 40:72; 63:41]

ELDREDGE, Thomas & 1/wf Mary STEBBINS (1642/3-by 1684); m bef 1668 Boston [TAG 41:95-6]

ELKINS, Oliver (c1660-c1723) & Jane PURCHASE (c1663-1716); m c1686 Lynn [TG 3:54]

ELLIS, John[3] (c1680-1758) & Sarah HOLMES (c1682-1762); m 7 Nov 1700 Plymouth [REG 120:26]

ELLIS, Manoah[2] (c1659-) & Mary[3] ?BURGESS; m c1679 Sandwich [REG 119:267]

ELLIS, Matthias[2] (1657-1748) & Mercy _____ (not NYE) (-1744+); m bef 1679 Sandwich/Yarmouth [REG 119:262, 125:140]

ELLIS, William[2] (c1665-1716) & Lydia ?BRIGGS (-1734+); m c1696 Middleborough [REG 119:271]

EMERY, John[1] & 1/wf Alice GRANTHAM; m 26 June 1620 Whiteparish, co Wilts/Newbury [TAG 65:213]

ENSIGN, Thomas[1] (c1605-) & 1/wf Anne WYBORNE (-bef 1639); m 27 Apr 1629 Cranbrook, Eng/Scituate [TAG 56:219, 60:99]

ENSIGN, Thomas[1] (c1605-) & 2/wf Elizabeth WILDER; m aft 1639, Scituate [TAG 60:99]

ERRINGTON, William (1592-) & Anne LIDDELL (bp 1598-1653); m 16 Sep 1619 All Saints, Newcastle/Cambridge [REG 132:49]

ESTOW, William[1] (c1600-1655) & Mary ( ) MOULTON; m 15 July 1623 Ormsby, Norfolk, Eng/Hampton [REG 142:259]

EVANS, Gilbert & Mercy HARKER; m bef 1680s Boston [Suffolk Deed 12:282]

EVELETH, Isaac[3] & 1/wf Sarah[4] PERKINS, dau of Jacob [AMacE]

EVELETH, Sylvester[1] (bp 1603/4-1688/9) & 1/wf Susan NUBERY (c1607-1659); m 21 Sep 1630 Exeter, co Devon [REG 134:299]

FARNHAM, Henry[1] (-1700) & Joan[2] (RUCK) (SWAN) HALSEY (bp 1620/1-1689); dau of Thomas[1] & Elizabeth; w of Henry; div wife of George; m bef 3 Dec 1662 Roxbury/Killingworth [TAG 62:35]

FARRINGTON, Edward & Elizabeth NEWHALL; m 29 Nov 1613 Sherington, co Bucks/Lynn [TAG 65:67]

FASSETT, John (-by 1736) & Mary[3] HILL (1667-1749); m 31 Mar 1697 Billerica [NGSQ 72:11]

FAWER, Barnabus (-by 1654/5) & Grace NEGUS (poss bp 1603/4-1671); m2 John JOHNSON; m bef 10 Mar 1643/4 Boston/Dorchester [TG 6:196]

FAYERWEATHER, Thomas (1661-bef 1694) & Hannah ( ) ELIOT (c1664-1717), w of Asaph; m c1689 Boston [REG 144:16]

FELT, Jonathan (c1672-1702) & Elizabeth (WILLIAMS) PURCHASE, w of Thomas Jr. (-1702+); m 3 Jan 1694/5 Salem [TG 3:56]

FENNER, Arthur[1] & Sarah BROWNE; m bef 1622 Ifield, co Sussex/RI [TAG 44:126]

FERN, John & Susannah COATS; m 25 June 1695 Lynn [REG 144:54]

FIFIELD, John[3] (-c1748) & 1/wf Abigail[3] WEARE (1676-1701+); m bef 1698 Hampton [TAG 55:18-19, 59:93]

FISH, Nathan & Deborah BARROWS; m 20 Dec 1687 Plymouth [TAG 60:159; MD 13:203]

FISH, Thomas[2] (-c1684) & Grissell STRANGE (c1650-); m2 Samuel[2] CORNELL; m 10 Dec 1668 Portsmouth [TAG 54:25]

FISHER, Joshua & 2/wf Anne ORSOR (not LUSON); m 7 Feb 1638/9 Syleham, co Suffolk [RCA]

FISHER, Thomas & Elizabeth ALLIN; m 21 Sep 1629 Saxlingham juxta mare, co Norfolk [RCA]

FISKE, John & Lydia FLETCHER (1646/7-1730), m2 Nathaniel[2] HILL [NGSQ 72:8]

FLOUNDERS, Thomas (-1670) & Sarah GREENE; m bef 9 May 1670 Newport, RI [TAG 59:146]

FOBES, William & Martha _____; Little Compton [LCVR]

FORD, Andrew[2] (c1650/1-1725) & Abiah PIERCE? (c1654-1721-25); m c1679/80 Weymouth [REG 119:103]

FORD, Nathaniel[2] (1658-1733) & Joanna[3] BICKNELL (1663-1739); m c1682 Weymouth [REG 119:110]

FOSKETT, John[1] & 1/wf Elizabeth LEACH; m bef 1670 Charlestown [TAG 43:37]

FOSTER, Samuel & Margery ( ) PITTS; m bef 30 Dec 1692 Salem [REG 144:545]

FOUNELL, John (c1607-1672/3) & Mary BROWNE (c1611-1696); m2 William HUDSON; m 18 Apr 1633 Hertford, co Herts./Charlestown [TAG 40:29-30]

FREAME, Thomas (c1650-1708+) & Mary ROWELL (1649/50-1708+); m 18 Sep 1673 Amesbury [TAG 55:44]

FRENCH, John & Deliverance CHUBB; m bet 1656-61 Gloucester [RCA]

FRENCH, Joseph & Sarah EASTMAN (1655-1748), m2 Solomon[2] SHEPARD [ASBO, p.374]

FRENCH, Samuel[2] & 2/wf Esther[2] (JACKMAN) MUZZEY; w of Joseph[2]; m3 John SWEEET; m c1682/3 Newbury [AMacE]

FROST, John[2] & Mehitabel BUTTOLPH (1651-1678); m 1 June 1668 Boston [TAG 58:132]

FULKE, John & _____; m 1661 Scituate [VR per PCRG]

FULLER, Joshua & Hannah[2] (GRIGGS) RAINSFORD (1659-), w of David [TAG 56:174; REG 139:307]

FULLER, Samuel (c1629-1695) & 2/wf Elizabeth (NICHOLAS) BOWEN (c1637-1713), w of Thomas; m c1660s Plympton/Middleborough [MD 39:86]

GAINES, Henry & Jane PARTRIDGE; m 17 May 1634 Olney, co Bucks/ Lynn [TAG 65:68]

GAUNT, Hannaniah[2] & Dorothy BUTLER (1650-   ); m 10 3mo 1678 Sandwich [REG 127:22, NGSQ 62:252]

GAY, John (-1688) & Joan (   ) BORDEN (-1691); w of John; m bef 1638 Dedham [REG 130:39]

GAY, Samuel[3] (1662/3-1753) & Mary CURTIS? (1667-1744); m c1687 Roxbury/Swansey [TG 1:77]

GAYLORD, William[1] (1582-   ) & Jone ASHWOOD; m 11 June 1610 Long Sutton, co Somerset/Dorchester [TAG 58:220]

GEE, John[1] (c1635-1702) & Mary _____ (-1703+) Eastchester [NYGBR 113:65]

GEE, Joseph[2] (1676-1716) & 1/wf Sarah ?LANCASTER (-c1700); Eastchester [NYGBR 113:65]

GEER, Daniel[2] & 1/wf Hannah _____ (-by 1728); m bef 1700 Preston [REG 142:46]

GEER, Joseph (1664-1743) & 1/wf Sarah HOWARD (1668-by 1713); m 17 Jan 1692/3 Preston [TAG 49:27]

GEORGE, John[1] (bp 1673-1715/6) & Ann[1] SWADDOCK (c1670s-1763); m 5 Nov 1698 St. James Pockthorpe, Norwich/Haverhill [ASBO, p.277]

GIBBS, Giles[1] & 2/wf Katherine CARWITHE; m 13 Apr 1629 St. Sidwell/Dorchester [TAG 61:33]

GIBBS, John[2] (1644-1725) & 1/wf Jane[2] BLACKWELL (c1650-1711-16); m c1669 Sandwich [REG 117:183, 123:56]

GIBBS, Samuel & 2/wf Patience BUTLER (1648-   ); m 5 Mar 1676 Sandwich [REG 127:22]

GIDDINGS, Joseph & Elizabeth ROSS; m bef 29 Mar 1698 [REG 144:54]

GILBERT, John (bp 1644-1673) & Sarah GREGSON (c1646-1697); m 12 Dec 1667 New Haven [REG 128:73]

GILLETTE, Jonathan (after 1640-   ) & Mercy BARBER; m c1680s Windsor, CT [TAG 45:225]

GILMAN, Edward & Elizabeth[2] SMITH, ?m2 Samuel DUDLEY [AMacE]

GILMAN, John & Hannah ?ROBINSON; m 9 Jan 1684/5 Hampton [TAG 55:18]

GLOVER, Henry (1610-1689) & Ellen RUSSELL; m bef 1652 [TAG 48:214]

GODFREY, William[3] (1672-1741-3) & Priscilla[2] ANNIS (1677-1768); m 17 Jan 1699/1700 Hampton [ASBO, p.125]

GOODRIDGE, Daniel[3] (1670-1747) & Mary[2] ORDWAY (1673-1754); m int 16 Nov 1698 Newbury [ASBO, p.90]

GOZZARD, Nicholas & Elizabeth[2] GILLETTE (1639-1699+); m c1671 Simsbury [TAG 56:130]

GRAY, John (-bef 1663) & Elizabeth[2] (FROST) WATSON (bp 1614-bef 1682); w of John; m bet 1634-9 CT [TAG 64:163]

GREEN, Samuel & Hannah BUTLER; m bef 1677 Hartford [TAG 46:11]

GREENLAND, David & Elizabeth BALLENTINE (1659-), m2 Roger YELLINGS, m3 John COOMBS [TAG 46:130]

GREENLEAF, Edmund[1] (-1671) & 1/wf Sarah MOORE; m 2 Jul 1611 Langford, co Essex/Salisbury [TAG 56:107, REG 122:28]

GREENLEAF, Edmund & Sarah (JURDAIN) (HILL) SOWTHER, w of William, w of Nathaniel [TAG 42:218]

GRIFFIN, Jonathan (-1685) & Mary LONG (c1650s-1720/1+); m2 Daniel[1] MUSSILLOWAY; m 25 Oct 1676 Sudbury [ASBO, p.165]

GROSS, Edmund[3] (-1727/8) & Martha DAMON (not BACON)(- 1730+); m 21 Apr __ Boston [REG 127:116]

GURNEY, Samuel & Sarah (ATKINS) STAPLES (c1651/2-c1724), w of John[2], m3 Richard WILLIAMS [REG 121:243]

GUY, Nicholas & Jane (_____) TAINTER; m license Upton Grey, co Hants 30 Oct 1629 [TAG 65:22]

HACKETT, William[1] & 2/wf Mary[2] ATKINS (b c1642-); m bef 1666 Dover [REG 121:242]

HALL, Joseph[2] (1642-1716) & 2/wf Mary JOYCE (c1644-1717/8), Mansfield, CT [TAG 43:3]

HALL, Samuel (1665-1750) & Hannah SAWTELL (1670-1753); m bef 1698 Stow/Groton/Concord [REG 126:6]

HALL, Thomas & Martha (DAVIES) (RUSSELL) BRADSHAW (-1695), w of William, w of Humphrey [TAG 44:83]

HALL, _____ & Mary BENSON (c1637-); m bef 1700 Hull [REG 142:270]

HALSEY, George & Joan^2 (RUCK) SWAN, w of Henry, m3 Henry^1 FARNHAM [TAG 62:35]

HAMLIN, Giles & 1/wf Bridget HARRIS; m bef 1655 [TAG 46:138]

HAMLIN, Giles (1622-1689) & 2/wf Esther CROW (-1700); m bef 1663 Hartford [TAG 46:138]

HAMMOND, _____ & Abigail SOMES (1655-1700+); m bef 1700 Boston [TAG 53:13]

HARDY, Jacob^2 (c1649-1706) & Lydia^2 EATON (1662-1737); m c1690 Bradford [ASBO, p.288]

HARDY, William^2 (c1644-c1722) & 1/wf Ruth TENNY (1653/4-1689); m 3 May 1678 Bradford [ASBO, p.287]

HARDY, William^2 (c1644-c1722) & 2/wf Sarah SAVORY (c1666-1762); m c1689 Bradford [ASBO, p.287]

HARLOCK, Thomas & Bethia MAYHEW, m2 Richard WAY [TAG 61:256]

HARRIS, George & Joan _____, m2 Thomas TUCK; m bef 1650 [EIHC 7:25]

HARRIS, John & Amie ____ (probably not HILLS); m 1656 Charlestown [REG 120:74]

HARRIS, ?Joseph (c1630-) & _____ CHUBB, dau of Thomas; m bef 24 Nov 1669 [EQC 4:216]

HARRIS, Richard (1618-28-1666) & _____ SMITH (c1618-23 -); dau of Richard^1; m Hartford [TAG 46:137]

HAWTHORNE, Nathaniel (-bef 1710) & Sarah HIGGINSON (1682-1750); m2 Nathaniel^3 SAWTELL; m 22 June 1699 Salem [REG 126:11]

HEATH, John^2 (1643-1706) & Sarah^2 PARTRIDGE (1647-1718); m 14 Nov 1666 Haverhill [ASBO, p.313]

HEATH, John^3 (1676-1731+) & Hannah^2 HAINES (-1731+); m 16 Dec 1697 Haverhill/Norwich [ASBO, p.316]

HEATH, Joseph^2 (c1645-1672) & Martha^2 DOW (1649-1707+); m2 Joseph^2 PAGE; m 27 June 1672 Haverhill [ASBO, p.314]

HEATH, Josiah[2] (1651-1731+) & 1/wf Mary[3] DAVIS (1647-1691+); m 19 Jul 1671 Haverhill [ASBO, p.315]

HEATH, William[1] (-1652) & 1/wf Mary CRAMPHORNE (-1624); m 10 Feb 1616/7 Great Amwell, Herts/Roxbury [REG 132:20]

HEATH, William[1] (-1652) & 2/wf Mary PERRY (?1602-); m 22 Jan 1622/3 Gilston, Herts/Roxbury [REG 132:20]

HERRICK, Henry[2] (-1702) & Lydia ?GROVER, dau of Edmund[1]; m Beverly [AMacE]

HEWES, John (c1653-1721) & Ruth SAWTELL (c1650-1720); m 9 Mar 1676/7 Watertown/Lexington [REG 126:5]

HENDRICK, Daniel & 1/wf Dorothy[2] PIKE (-1659); m bef 1645 Haverhill [REG 121:162]

HILL, Jonathan[2] (1646-1710+) & Mary HARTWELL (c1643-1694/5); m 11 Dec 1666 Billerica [NGSQ 72:10]

HILL, Nathaniel[2] (c1642-1706) & 1/wf Elizabeth HOLMES (1644-1685); m 21 June 1667 Billerica [NGSQ 72:8]

HILL, Nathaniel[2] (c1642-1706) & 2/wf Lydia (FLETCHER) FISKE (1646/7-1730), w of John; m after 1685 Billerica [NGSQ 72:8]

HILL, Ralph (-1663) & 2/wf Margaret ( ) TOOTHAKER (aft 1597-1683); m 21 Dec 1638 Plymouth Colony [NGSQ 72:6]

HILL, Ralph (bef 1633-1695) & Martha TOOTHAKER (c1636-1703/4); m 15 Nov 1660 Billerica [NGSQ 72:6]

HILL, Roger[1] (c1640s-bef 1710) & 1/wf Ann _____ (-1682/3); m bef 1676 Bedminster, Eng.\Beverly [ASBO, p.334]

HILL, Roger[1] (c1640s-bef 1710) & 2/wf Elizabeth _____ (-aft 1721); m bef 1689 Beverly [ASBO, p.334]

HILL, Samuel[3] (1671/2-1762) & Sarah PAGE (-1758); m claimed 7 Jan 1698/9 Billerica [NGSQ 72:17]

HILL, William & Sarah JURDAIN, m2 Nathaniel SOWTHER, m3 Edmund GREENLEAF [TAG 42:218]

HILLS, Joseph & Ann ( ) LUNT, w of Henry[1] [Abel Lunt, p.5]

HINGSTON, George[1] (bp 1631-1667) & Alice **GREENSLADE**; m 25 Oct 1660 Newton Ferrers/Boston [REG 125:202]

HOAR, Hezekiah[1] (bp 1608-c1692) & Rebecca _____ (c1630-1679+); m c1653 Taunton [REG 141:32]

HOBBY, John & Sarah **GRAY** (c1642-   ); m c1662 [TAG 64:167]

HOLLINGSWORTH, Richard (c1594-5-1654) & 1/wf _____; m bef 1626 Eng [TAG 40:77]

HOLLINGSWORTH, Richard (c1594-5-1654) & 2/wf Susan ?**HUNTER**; m c1626/7 Eng [TAG 40:77]

HOLLOWAY, Joseph[3] (c1668-1732) & Ann **JENNINGS** (1670-1732+); m c1693 Sandwich [NGSQ 64:20]

HOLMAN, Edward (1647?-   ) & Richard[2] (female) **BRIMBLECOM** (1646-) (not **HOOPER**); m c1665 Marblehead [DCD]

HOLMES, Francis (c1670s-1726) & Rebecca **WHARF** (c1670s-1730/1); m 11 Feb 1693/4 Boston [TG 3:57]

HOLMES, John[2] (c1636-1697) & 1/wf Patience **FAUNCE** (c1640-bef 1681); m 20 Nov 1661 Plymouth [NGSQ 74:87]

HOLMES, John[2] (c1636-1697) & 2/wf Patience **(BONHAM) WILLIS** (c1647-1724+), w of Richard; m c1681 Plymouth [NGSQ 74:87]

HOLMES, John & 1/wf Elizabeth[3] **GATES** (1671-1726); m c1690 Stow [REG 120:164]

HOLMES, Samuel[1] (bef 1651-1690/1) & 2/wf Mary _____ (c1655-1722+); m2 Peter **CHENEY** Jr.; m c1678-81 Boston [ASBO, p.341]

HOLYOKE, Edward[1] & Prudence **STOCKTON**; m 17 June 1612 Kimcote, Leicestershire [NGSQ 69:11]

HOMER, Michael & Mary (   ) **BURROUGHS**, w of George; m3 Christopher **HALL** [TAG 56:43]

HORSINGTON, John[1] (c1640s-1703) & 1/wf _____ (-c1688-93); m c1680 Wethersfield [REG 141:40]

HORSINGTON, John[1] (1640s-1703) & 2/wf Mary **(STANBOROUGH) EDWARDS** (-1728); m c1688-93 CT [REG 141:40]

HOSKINS, Anthony & Mary (**GRIFFEN**) **WILSON**, w of Samuel; m bef 7 Mar 1700/1 Windsor, CT [TAG 52:80]

HOUGH, Samuel (1653-1718) & 1/wf Hannah **ORVIS** (1655-c1678); m c1676 Wallingford [TAG 41:46]

HOUGH, Samuel (1653-1718) & 2/wf Susanna **WROTHAM** [TAG 41:46]

HOUGH, Samuel (1653-1718) & 3/wf Mary **BATES** [TAG 41:46]

HOWCHEN, Jerimy & Hester **PIGEON**; 16 Aug 1636 Pulham St Mary the Virgin, co Norfolk [RCA]

HOWLAND, Arthur[1] (-1675) & Margaret ( ) **WALKER** (-1683); m "possibly long before" 6 June 1643 Fen Stanton, Hunts/Plymouth/ Marshfield [NGSQ 71:84]

HOWLETT, John (-1679+) & Abigail **POWELL** (c1651-); m bef 1671 Boston [REG 131:174]

HOXIE, Gideon[2] & Grace **GIFFORD** (1671-1714+); m c1695 Sandwich [REG 128:254]

HOYT/HOYLE, John[3] (1663-1691) & Elizabeth[2] **CHALLIS** (bef 1671-1744+); m2 John[3] **BLAISDELL**; m c1685 Amesbury [ASBO, p.151]

HUBBARD/HOBART, Peter & Elizabeth **IBROOK**; m 12 Oct 1628 Covehithe, co Suffolk [RCA]

HUBBARD, Jeremiah & Elizabeth **WHITING**, dau of Samuel; m c1620s Eng [TAG 40:81]

HUDSON, William & Mary (**BROWNE**) **FOUNELL** (c1611-1696), w of John [TAG 40:29]

HULING, Walton (-1710+) & Martha **PALMER** (-1718+); Newport, RI [TAG 60:159]

HULLING, Josiah/Jesse? & ____ ____; m 11 Jan 1675 New Shoreham, RI [TAG 60:159]

HUNT, Richard & Jane _____ (-1652), m2 William[1] **TING** [NGSQ 69:115]

HUNTING, John[1] (-1696) & Hester **SEABORNE** (-bet 1675/6-84); m 28 June 1624 Wramplingham, co Norfolk/Dedham [NGSQ 74:4]

HURD, Adam[1] & _____ _____ (-bef 1671) not Hannah BARTRAM; m bef 1640 Stratford, CT [TAG 50:5]

HURD, John (c1613-1681) & 2/wf Sarah THOMPSON (-1717/8); m2 Thomas BARNUM; m 10 Dec 1662 Stratford [TAG 50:3]

HURD, John, Jr. & Anna[2] (TUTTLE) JUDSON, w of Joshua[2] [TAG 50:7]

HURD, Joseph[2] (1644-by 1693) & Sarah ?LONG (-1693); m bef 1667 Boston [REG 132:86]

HUSSEY, Richard[2] & Jane[3] CANNEY; m c1691 Dover [AMacE]

HUTCHINS, Joseph[2] (1641-1689) & Joanna[2] CORLISS (1650-1734); m2 Stephen[2] DOW; m 29 Dec 1669 Haverhill [ASBO, p.210]

HUTCHINS, William[2] (1638-by 1691) & 1/wf Sarah[2] HARDY (c1637-1684); m 1 Jul 1661 Haverhill [ASBO, p.287]

HUTCHINSON, Joseph (c1633-1716) & 1/wf Bethiah CLARKE/PRINCE? (bp 1638-bef 1678); m bef 1660, Salem, MA [TAG 39:111]

HUTCHINSON, Richard & Alice BOSWORTH; m bef 1633 Salem [TAG 39:111]

ILSLEY, William (1612-1681) & Barbara STEVENS (1611-1681+); m 6 Mar 1637/8 Caversham, co Oxford/Newbury [TAG 50:61]

INGALLS, Edmund (c1588-1648) & Annis TELBE (-1649+); m 7 June 1618 Church of St Nicholas, Skirbeck, co Lincoln/Ipswich, MA [TAG 52:242]

INION, John, & Question? TYLER (c1665-72-   ); m bef 1697, Portsmouth, RI [TAG 52:221]

JACKSON, John[1] (bp 1608-1666) & 1/wf Elinor MILCOME; m 10 Aug 1629 Dartmouth, St. Saviour/Portsmouth [REG 144:33]

JACKSON, John[1] (bp 1608-1666) & 2/wf Joane LURFETE (c1612-bef 1680); m 30 Mar 1633 Portsmouth, NH [REG 144:33]

JACKSON, John[1] (bp 1624-1682+) & Sarah PALMER; m 27 Apr 1654 Dartmouth, Eng [REG 144:37]

JACKSON, Walter & 1/wf Jane _____; m bef 1666, Dover [TAG 53:134]

JACKSON, Walter (-1697/8) & 2/wf Ann _____; m aft 1666, Dover [TAG 53:134]

JACOBS, George[1] & 1 or 2/wf Mary JACOBS; m bef 12 Jan 1673/4 Salem [TAG 58:71]

JAMES, William[1] (c1650-1697) & Susannah MARTIN (-1726); m 10 Dec 1677 Newport [REG 126:247]

JAY, Joseph & Mary PRINCE; m bef 1689 Hingham [TAG 56:246]

JENNEY, Samuel & 1/wf Susanna WOOD (-1654); Plymouth/Dartmouth [TAG 60:159]

JENNINGS, John (-bef 1723) & Ruhama TURNER (c1645-bef 1723); m 29 6mo 1667 Sandwich [NGSQ 64:19]

JOHNSON, David (-by 1 Mar 1635/6) & _____; Dorchester [RCA]

JOHNSON, John & Grace (NEGUS) FAWER (poss. bp 1603/4-1671), w of Barnabus [TG 6:196]

JOHNSON, Joseph (1637-1714) & 1/wf Mary SAWTELL (1640-1664/5); m 19 Apr 1664 Charlestown [REG 126:5]

JONES, Richard (-1670) & Elizabeth CARPENTER (1644-1694+); m2 John CHAPPELL div; m3 _____ HILL; m c1662 Haddam [TAG 41:42]

JONES, Thomas & Ann (PRIDDETH) WOOD, w of Richard, m3 Paul WHITE [REG 139:141]

JORDAN, ____ & Susannah _____; m bef 1693 Marblehead [LB]

JUDSON, Joshua[2] & Anna[2] TUTTLE (1632/3-); m2 John HURD Jr.; m bef 1655 Stratford [TAG 50:7]

KEENE, John (c1621-c1675) & Hannah STEBBINS (1640-by 1685); m bef 1660 Boston [TAG 41:95]

KEILAM, Augustine & Alice GORBALL; m 8 Sep 1619 Wrentham, Suffolk [RCA]

KELLY, James & Susanna CLARK, m2 Nathaniel SANFORD, m3 John BUTTOLPH [TAG 58:136]

KELSEY, John & Hannah (not Phebe) DESBOROUGH; bef 1670 Hartford [TAG 38:210]

KENRICK, John & 1/wf Anna ?SAWTELL (-1656); m bef 1651 Muddy River [REG 126:1]

KETTEL, Nathan (-1723) & Hannah **EVELETH** (bp 1643-1670); m 1669 Boston/Gloucester [REG 134:309]

KEYSER, George & Rebecca **(AYER) ASLEBEE** (-bef 1702), w of John; m after 1671 [TAG 40:231]

KIMBALL, Henry & Susanna (probably not **STONE) CUTTING** (-1684) w of Richard; m3 Thomas **LOW**; m 27 Nov 1628 Mistley, co Essex [TAG 55:26]

KIND, Arthur (c1611-1686/7) & Jane _____ (c1624-1710); m bef 1646 Boston [REG 126:17]

KINDE, John^2 (c1646-1690) & Rachel _____ (-1690); m bef 1674 Boston [REG 126:19]

KING, William & Deborah **PRINCE**, m2 Robert **SMITH** [TAG 59:232]

KINGSBURY, Samuel^2 (c1649/50-1698) & Huldah^2 **CORLISS** (1661-   ); m2 Abraham^2 **WHITTAKER**; m 5 Nov 1679 Haverhill [ASBO, p.212]

KIRTLAND, Philip (bp 1611-   ) & Rose _____; Olney, co Bucks/Lynn [TAG 65:66-7]

LADD, Samuel^2 (1649-1697/8) & Martha^2 **CORLISS** (1652/3-1697+); m 1 Dec 1674 Haverhill [ASBO, p.211]

LANCASTER, John (c1670-1717) & Sarah (   ) **BANKS** (c1660-5-1740/1); m c1697 Eng [TAG 50:11]

LANDERS, Joseph^2 (c1666-c1750) & Rebecca (   ) **ALLEN**, w of John^4 [REG 124:45]

LANDERS, Richard^2 (c1660-c1750) & Sarah^3 **FREEMAN** (1662-1732/3); m 6 Jan 1695/6 Sandwich [REG 124:49]

LANDERS, Thomas^2 (c1658-1730/1) & Deborah **FREEMAN** (1665-1732+); m c1688 Sandwich [REG 124:46]

LANGFORD, Thomas (bp 1634-1670 & Mary **COOK** (c1650-1670/1); m bef 1670 Portsmouth, RI [Fiske 1:32]

LEACH, Peter & Hannah **RAINSFORD** (1671-1721+); m c1693 Boston [REG 139:304]

LEE, Peter & Ann **MOSHER**; m bef 1690 E. Greenwich, RI [TAG 59:239]

LETTIN, Richard[1] (bp 1608/9-1673) & 1/wf Joan CHADD; m 3 Nov 1634 Salford co Bedford/Oyster Bay [NYGBR 117:222]

LETTIN, Richard[1] (bp 1608/9-1673) & 2/wf Joan ( ) IRELAND; m license 24 August 1670 Oyster Bay [NYGBR 117:222]

LINDLEY, John & 1/wf Ellen DAYTON (bp 1626-1654); m c1644-5 New Haven [REG 128:148]

LINNELL, Robert & 1/wf _____; Barnstable [TAG 51:35]

LINNELL, Robert & 2/wf Peninah HOWES; m bet 1623-1638 Barnstable [TAG 51:35]

LONGLEY, William Jr. (-1694) & Deliverance CRISPE (c1650-1694); m bef Apr 1674 Groton [TAG 62:27]

LORESEN, Cornelius & Abiel PAIGE; m 25 Oct 1697 Boston [TAG 132:38]

LOUNSBURY, Richard[2] (c1672-1715) & Abigail THOMAS (1674-bef 1733), dau of John; m c1690s New Haven/NYC [NYGBR 99:65]

LOVETT, Thomas & Bethiah STANDLY; m bef 26 Dec 1693 Beverly [REG 144:54]

LOW, Thomas & Susanna ( ) (CUTTING) KIMBALL (-1684), w of Richard, w of Henry [TAG 55:26]

LUDLOW, Roger (-1666) & Mary COGAN (-bef 1666); m c1620 Chard, co Somerset/Fairfield [NGSQ 51:233]

LUGG, John & Jane DEIGHTON, m2 Jonathan NEGUS [TG 6:195]

LUMBART, Thomas (bp 1581-1663-4) & 2/wf Joyce _____ (-1683+); m bef 1630 Dorchester/Barnstable [TAG 52:136]

LUNT, Henry[1] (c1610-1662) & Ann _____ (c1620-1688+); m2 Joseph HILLS; m c1638 Newbury [Abel Lunt, p.5]

LUNT, Henry[2] (1652-1709) & Jane BROWNE (c1657-1737+); m2 Joseph MAYO; m c1676 Newbury [Abel Lunt, p.13]

LUSHER, Eleazar & Anna BANCRAFTE; m 8 Jul 1628 Pulham St Mary the Virgin, Norfolk [RCA]

MACOMBER, William (1610-1670) & Ursula COOPER; m 16 Jan 1633/4 St Mary's, Bridport, co Dorset [TG 2:170]

MAGOUN, James (1666-bef 1705) & 1/wf Sarah FORD (1672-1735+); m c1695 Duxbury [REG 119:14]

MAHURIN, Hugh[1] (-1718) & Mary ?CAMPBELL; m2 William BASSETT; m bef 1691 Taunton [REG 136:18]

MANN, Thomas[2] (1650-1732) & Sarah ENSIGN; m c1678 Scituate [TAG 61:48]

MARCH, Hugh (1673-1695) & Sarah COKER (1676-1717/8); m2 Archelaus ADAMS; m c1694 [Abel Lunt, p.48]

MARTYN, Richard & Elizabeth SALTER; m 9 June 1630 Ottery St Mary, co Devon [REG 127:28]

MARTIN, Robert & Joanna UPHAM; m 16 Nov 1618 Ottery St Mary, co Devon [REG 127:28]

MASON, John[2] & Abigail FITCH (1650-) [TAG 40:54]

McALLISTER, Angus (c1670-1737+) & Margaret _____; m bef 1698 Northern Ireland/Londonderry, NH [NGSQ 68:165]

MENDALL, John & ____ (HEWES) BURROUGHS, w of Jeremiah; m bef 1663 Marshfield [TAG 40:33]

MERRILL, Abel[2] (1643/4-1689) & Priscilla[2] CHASE (1648/9-1697+); m 10 Feb 1670/1 Newbury [ASBO, p.173]

MERRILL, John[1] & Elizabeth VINCENT; m 15 July 1633 Little Wenham, co Suffolk/Newbury [HQ 24:38]

MERRITT, John (1661-1740) & Elizabeth PINCEN (1663/4-1746) not HYLAND; m c1686 Scituate [TAG 50:98]

MINGAY, Geafry & Anne CAPEN; m 30 Sep 1630 Denton, Norfolk [RCA]

MONROE, John (-1691) & Sarah ____; m bef 1667, Bristol, MA [TAG 40:201]

MOON, Ebenezer & Rebecca PEABODY; m bef 1686 [REG 117:97]

MOORE, John & 2/wf Elizabeth RICE (bp 1612-); m bef 1639 Sudbury [TG 6:139]

MORE, Richard (1614-1698/9) & 1/wf Christian HUNTER (c1615-1676); m 20 Oct 1636 Plymouth/Salem [TAG 40:79]

MORE, William & Mary (?**CROWELL**) **ALLEN** (-1727), w of Joshua; nd [REG 125:232-4]

MOREY, Jonathan[3] (-c1733) & Hannah **BOURNE** (1667-1732), m 24 Jan 1689 Plymouth [REG 118:199]

MORSE, Joseph (1671-1709) & Elizabeth **SAWTELL** (1671-1713/4+); m2 Benjamin **NOURSE**; m 25 Aug 1691 Watertown [REG 126:7]

MORTON, Ephraim[4] (1671-) & Hannah[3] **FAUNCE** (1678-); m2 John **COOK**; m c1698 Plymouth [REG 116:119]

MULFORD, John (1670-1730) & 1/wf Jemima **HIGGENS** (-1723); m 1 Nov 1699 Eastham [TAG 40:197]

MULFORD, Thomas (c1640-1706) & 1/wf Elizabeth **BARNS** (bp 1644-by 1678/9); m bef 1670 Hingham [TAG 40:193]

MUNROE, John[1] & Sarah _____ (-1692/3); m bef 1670 Scotland/Bristol, RI [TAG 61:181]

MUSSILOWAY, Daniel[1] (c1645-1710/11) & 2/wf Mary (**LONG**) **GRIFFIN** (c1650s-1720/1+), w of Jonathan; m 7 Sep 1687 Newbury [ASBO, p.165]

MUZZEY, Joseph & Esther **JACKMAN**, m2 Samuel **FRENCH**; m3 John **SWEET** [AMacE]

NEALE, Francis[1] (c1626-bef 1697) & Jane **ANDREWS** (1629/30-1686+); m bef 28 Mar 1658 [TG 3:51]

NEFF, William[1] (c1639-42-1688/9) & Mary[2] **CORLISS** (1646-1722); m 23 Jan 1665/6 Haverhill [ASBO, p.210]

NEGUS, Benjamin (c1612-by 1693/4) & Elizabeth **WILLIAMSON** (c1612-1681/2); m St Faith the Virgin, London aft 22 Feb 1637/8 [TG 6:198]

NEGUS, Jabez (bp 1648-1723) & 1/wf Hannah **PHILLIPS** (1643-by1693/4); m bef 28 Sep 1674 Boston [TG 6:201]

NEGUS, Jabez (bp 1648-1723) & 2/wf Sarah **BROWN** (-1737+); m 9 Jan 1693/4 Boston [TG 6:201]

NEGUS, Jonathan (c1601-1675/6) & Jane (**DEIGHTON**) **LUGG** (bp 1609-1671+), w of John; m bef 27 Oct 1647 Boston [TG 6:195]

NELSON, Thomas[1] (-1648) & 1/wf Dorothy **STAPLETON** (-1637); m 1626 Yorkshire [REG 128:82]

NELSON, William[1] (c1635-bef 1694) & Elizabeth[2] CROSS (1636-1694+); m by 1658 Ipswich [ASBO, p.229]

NEWCOMBE, Francis (?1592-1692) & Rachel BRACKETT (1615-); m 27 May 1630 Sudbury/Boston [TAG 52:92, 55:215]

NEWCOMB, John[2] (1634-1722) & Ruth MARSHALL (-1697); m bef 1659 Braintree [TAG 61:113]

NEWHALL, Anthony & Mary WHITE; m 6 Nov 1632 Olney, co Bucks/ Lynn [TAG 65:66]

NEWHALL, Thomas & Mary WOOD[ARD?]; m 12 Jun 1618 Clifton Beynes, co Bucks/Lynn [TAG 65:66]

NEWTON, Richard[1] & Anna LOKER; m 1636 Bures St. Mary [TAG 55:87]

NORTHWAY, John & Susanna (BRIGGS) PALMER; m bef 1684 Portsmouth, RI [TAG 60:159]

NUTT, Miles (bp 1598-1671) & 1/wf Sarah BRANSON; m 16 Jul 1623 Barking, co Suffolk [TAG 52:21]

OLIVER, Thomas & Bridget (PLAYFER) WASSILBE (-1692), w Samuel; m3 Edward BISHOP; m 26 July 1666 Salem [TAG 57:129-38; TAG 64:207]

ORDWAY, Edward[2] (1653-1714) & 1/wf Mary[2] WOOD (1653-1704); m 12 Dec 1678 Newbury [ASBO, p.91]

ORDWAY, Hannaniah[2] (1665-1758) & 1/wf Abigail MERRILL (1665-1708); m bef 1690 Newbury [ASBO, p.89]

ORDWAY, James[1] (bp 1621-c1710) & 1/wf Ann[2] EMERY (bp 1632/3-1686/7); m 25 Nov 1648 Newbury [ASBO, p.77]

ORDWAY, James[1] (bp 1621-c1710) & 2/wf Joanna (DAVIS) CORLISS (c1620s-1690s); w of George; m 4 Oct 1687 Newbury [ASBO, p.77]

ORDWAY, James[2] (1651-1721/2) & 2/wf Sarah CLARK (1675-); m 19 June 1696 Rowley [ASBO, p.87]

ORDWAY, Samuel[1] (-1692-4) & Sarah[2] ORDWAY (1655/6-1715+); m 25 Feb 16[78] Ipswich [ASBO, p.68]

PABODIE, William (1664-1744) & 1/wf Judith TILDEN (1669/70-1714); m 27 June 1693 Little Compton, RI [TAG 53:246-8]

PAGE, Joseph[2] & Martha[2] **(DOW) HEATH** (1649-1707+), w of Joseph[2] [ASBO, p.314]

PAGE, Robert[1] (1604-1679) & Lucy **WARD** (bp 1604/5-1665); m 8 Oct 1629 St Marys, So Walsham, Norfolk [REG 141:120]

PAINE, Stephen[1] (c1602-7-1679) & 1/wf Neele **ADCOCKE** (bp 1602/3-1660); m bef 1629 Norfolk/Hingham [TAG 62:107; REG 143:299]

PALMER, Samuel & Elizabeth **BOND**, m2 Ephraim[1] **CHILD** [TAG 62:29]

PALMER, William & Susanna **BRIGGS**; m2 John **NORTHWAY**; Plymouth/Little Compton [TAG 60:160]

PARKER, John & Mary **(?POPE) POULTER** (c1596-1692/3), w of John[1], m3 Thomas **CHAMBERLAIN** [REG 141:217]

PARKER, John (c1665-1744) & 1/wf Sarah **VERIN** (c1665-1711); m bef 1695 Boston [REG 131:110]

PARKER, Peter[2] & Sarah[3] **COOK** (c1646-aft 1675); m c1664 Portsmouth RI/Shrewsbury, NJ [Fiske p.45]

PARKER, Peter (c1668-1727) & Hannah _____ (-1760), m2 Joseph **CARPENTER**; Westerly, RI [Fiske 1:45]

PARKHURST, George & 1/wf Phebe **LEET**; m Eng/Watertown [TAG 52:113]

PARSEVAL, James (1671-1728) & 1/wf Abigail **ROBINSON** (1674-); m 27 Feb 1696 or 18 Feb 1695/6 Falmouth delete Parseuah [TAG 60:160; MD 30:59]

PARTRIDGE, William & Anne **SPIGON?**, m2 Anthony **STANYON**; m 5 Oct 1635? Olney co Bucks/Lynn [TAG 65:68]

PAULING, Matthew (-1708) & Sarah **(HUNTER) WALKER** (1663-1704-8); w of Samuel; m 15 June 1698 Boston [TAG 40:82]

PECK, Benjamin[2] (bp 1647-1730) & Mary **SPERRY** (1650-); m 29 Mar 1670 New Haven [REG 121:83]

PECK, Eleazer (bp 1648/9-1736) & 1/wf Mary **BUNNELL** (1650-1724); m 31 Oct 1671 New Haven/Wallingford [REG 121:84]

PECK, Joseph[2] (bp 1647-1720) & Sarah **ALLING** (bp 1649-1734); m 28 Nov 1672 New Haven [REG 121:83]

PEIRCE, William & Sarah KIND (1646-c1704/5); m2 Wm ROUSE; m 13 Jul 1666 Charlestown [REG 126:18]

PENNOYER, Samuel & Rose HOBSON (c1616-1698), m2 Samuel DESBOROW [NGSQ 60:248]

PENTICOAST, John[1] & 1/wf Joane (MILES) SMYTH; w of Richard; m 27 Nov 1632 Cranbrook, co Kent/Charlestown [TAG 62:118]

PERKINS, John[2] & Elizabeth ?WESTLY; m c1635 Ipswich? [AMacE]

PERRY, John[2] (1657-) & Elizabeth ?WILLIAMSON; dau of Timothy[1]; m bef 1684 Sandwich [REG 126:279]

PERRY, Seth[2] & 2/wf Dorothy POWELL (1643-); m bef 1665 Dedham [REG 131:174]

PETTINGILL, Nathaniel[2] (1654-c1717/8) & 1/wf Mary ____ (-bef 1703); m bef 1694 Newbury [Abel Lunt, p.53]

PETTINGILL, Samuel[2] (1644/5-1711) & Sarah POORE (-1716+); m 13 Feb 1673/4 Newbury [Abel Lunt, p.53]

PHELPS, Henry (-1670s) & 2/wf Hannah (BASKEL) PHELPS (bef 1630-1695+); w of Nicholas; m c1664 Salem [NGSQ 75:296]

PHELPS, Joseph & Hannah NEWTON, dau of Anthony; m 20 Sep 1660 Windsor [TAG 65:13-16]

PHELPS, Nicholas (-c1664) & Hannah BASKEL (bef 1630-1695+); m Salem c1650 [NGSQ 75:296]

PHELPS, William[1] (c1592-1672) & 1/wf Mary ____; m c1617 Crewkerne, co Somerset/Windsor [TAG 65:163]

PHELPS, William[1] (c1592-1672) & 2/wf Anne DOVER (-1675); m 14 Nov 1626 Crewkerne, co Somerset [TAG 65:163]

PHETTIPLACE, Philip (bp 1621-1687+) & ____; m bef 1682, RI [REG 123:252]

PHILBRICK, James[3] (c1679-bef 1707/8) & Sarah SILVER (1682-1770); m2 Benjamin[3] EMERSON; m c1700 Hampton [TAG 40:20]

PHIPPS, Solomon (c1619-1671) & Elizabeth WOOD (bp 1620-1688); m bef 15 3mo 1642 Charlestown [TG 9:91]

PIGGOT, Christopher & _____ _____; m bef 27 Apr 1655 Boston [RCA]

PIKE, John[2] (bp 1613-1689/90) & 1/wf Mary **TURVELL** (bp 1615/16-1680-5); m bef 1638 Hants/Wilts/Woodbridge [REG 121:162]

PIKE, John[2] (bp 1613-1689/90) & 2/wf Elizabeth **(BLOSSOM) FITZ-RANDOLPH** (-1690+); m 30 June 1685 Piscataway, NJ [REG 121:162]

PIKE, Moses[3] (1658-1741/2) & Susanna **WORCESTER** (1671-1710+); m bef 1688 Salisbury [REG 121:167]

PIKE, Thomas[3] (1657-1730) & 3/wf Mary **(HUNT) PHILLIPS** (-1730+); w of Ephraim; m 30 June 1699 Woodbridge, NJ [REG 121:165]

PINDER, Henry (-1661) & 1/wf Mary **ROGERS** (1582-); m 22 May 1614 Church of St. Mary the Great, Cambridge, Eng/Ipswich, MA [TAG 52:175]

PINSON, Thomas[1] & Joan ( ) **STANLEY**; w of Daniel[1]; m 4 Nov 1639 Scituate [TAG 50:97]

PINSON, Thomas[2] (1640-1714) & Elizabeth **WHITE** (1642-1714+) (only wife); m 18 Sep 1662 Scituate [TAG 50:98]

PINSON, Thomas[3] (1665-1733) & Sarah **(STOCKBRIDGE) TURNER** (1665-); w? of Israel; m 23 Feb 1691/2 or 26 Dec 1693 Scituate [TAG 50:99; 38:186]

PITCHER, John[2] (1650-) & 1/wf Hannah _____ (-c1690); m bef 1683 Boston [TAG 59:204]

PITCHER, John[2] (1650-) & 2/wf Mary _____ (-1703); m bef 1695 Boston [TAG 59:205]

PLUMB, John (c1634-) & Elizabeth **GREEN** (1640-); m bef 1666 Hartford [TAG 46:10]

POPE, Isaac & Alice **FREEMAN** (1658-1755); m c1686 Dartmouth [TAG 40:110]

PORTER, John[3] (1667-1723) & 1/wf Mercy **CARVER** (1672/3-1708/9); m c1693 Weymouth [REG 119:94]

POULTER, John[1] (c1596-1638) & Mary ?**POPE** (c1596-1692/3); m2 John **PARKER**; m3 Thomas **CHAMBERLAIN**; m c1630 Rayleigh, Essex, Eng/Chelmsford [REG 141:217]

POWELL, Michael[1] (c1605-bef 1672/3) & Abigail BEDLE (bp 1608-bef 1677); m c1630 Eng/Dedham [REG 131:173]

PRATT, Matthew & Elizabeth KINGMAN; m Ashton Clinton, Bucks. 9 Nov 1619 [TAG 65:89]

PRATT, Phinehas (1590-3-1680) & Mary PRIEST (-1682+); m c1627-33 Plymouth/Charlestown, MA [TAG 60:160]

PRESTON, Samuel & Abigail THOMAS delete [NYGBR 99:65]

PRICE, Theodore & Anne WOOD; m2 Dudley BRADSTREET [REG 139:139]

PURCHASE, Thomas (c1660-1681/2) & Elizabeth WILLIAMS (-1727+); m2 Jonathan FELT; m 3 Dec 1679 Salem [TG 3:53]

PURRIER, William & Alice KNIGHT; m 21 Feb 1621/2 Olney, co Bucks/ Ipswich/Southold [TAG 65:69]

PUTNAM, John & Priscilla GOULD; m bef 1605 Eng/Salem [REG 119:174]

RAINSFORD, David[2] (1644-1691) & 2/wf Hannah[2] GRIGGS (not Abigail)(1659-); m2 Joshua FULLER; m bef 1674 Boston [TAG 56:174, REG 139:307]

RAINSFORD, John[3] (1661/2-1710/11) & Rebecca ____; m2 1712 John NICHOLLS; m bef 1695 Boston [REG 139:311]

RAMSDEN, John & Elizabeth[2] (FROST) (WATSON) GRAY (bp 1614-bef 1682); w of John, w of John; m bef 1663 Newtown, LI [TAG 64:163]

RAYMOND, John & Martha[2] WOODIN (1654/5-); m bef 1677 Beverly [TAG 64:73]

REMINGTON, Daniel (1661-1690s) & Sarah[3] PARKER (c1670-1686); m c1685 RI [TAG 57:22; Fiske 1:46]

REMINGTON, Stephen (c1659-1738) & Penelope PARKER (1666-1740+); m c1685 Portsmouth, RI [TAG 57:20; Fiske 1:45]

RICHARDS, John & Mary FULLER; m2 Boaz BROWN [REG 140:317]

RICHARDSON, Joshua (c1651-bef 1724/5) & 2/wf Jane[2] ORDWAY (1663-1705+); m 4 Jan 1687/8 Newbury [ASBO, p.88]

RING, William (-c1620s) & Mary DURRANT? (-1631); m 21 May 1601 Ufford, co Suffolk/Plymouth, MA [TAG 42:193]

ROBINSON, John (1611/12-1675) & Elizabeth **PEMBERTON** (-1645); m by 1641 Newbury [REG 143:151]

ROGERS, Henry & Ann (   ) **WOOD**; w of George; m after 1664 LI [TAG 39:131]

ROGERS, Robert (c1617-1663) & Susanna ____ (-1677); m2 William **THOMAS**; m bef 1647/8 Newbury [REG 140:204]

ROGERS, Thomas[1] (-1638) & Grace (**RAVENS**) **SHERMAN**; w of John; m bef 1634 co Essex/Watertown [TAG 62:76]

ROOTS, Jurrian (-1697) & Willmet (   ) **ALBERTSON**; Oyster Bay [NYGBR 109:205]

ROSSITER, Edward[1] (c1575-1630) & _____ **COMBE?**; m bef 1599 Eng/ Dorchester [REG 138:12]

ROUND, John[1] (c1620-   ) & Ruth ____ (-1658/9); m c1646 Yarmouth [TAG 54:37]

ROUND, John[2] (c1646-1716) & Elizabeth **?CHASE**; m c1669 Yarmouth [TAG 54:37]

ROUSE, William (c1640-1704/5) & Sarah (**KIND**) **PEIRE** (1646-c1704/5); w of William; m bef 1676 Charlestown [REG 126:18]

ROWLEY, Henry & Anne (**HELSDON**) **BLOSSOM**; w Thomas [TAG 63:74]

RUSSELL, William[1] (-1661/2) & Martha **DAVIES** (-1695); m2 Humphrey **BRADSHAW**; m3 Thomas **HALL**; m 26 May 1636 Abbotts Langley, Herts [TAG 44:83]

ST. JOHN, Matthias/Matthew[1] (-1669?) & Mary ____ (-c1714); m by 1633 Eng/Dorchester/Windsor [TAG 60:160; 53:241]

SAMPSON, George (c1653-1739) & Elizabeth **SPRAGUE** (c1657-1727); m c1678 Plympton [TAG 41:189, 63:209]

SAMPSON, Isaac & Lydia **STANDISH**, m c1686 Plymouth [MD 39:127]

SANDERSON, Edward[1] (c1614-   ) & Mary **EGGLESTON** (not Sarah **LYNN**); m 16 Oct 1645 Watertown [REG 127:181]

SANDERSON, Jonathan[3] (1673-1743) & Abigail **FISKE** (1675-1759); m 14 Jul 1699 [REG 127:185]

SANFORD, Nathaniel & Susanna **(CLARK) KELLY**, w of James, m3 John[2] **BUTTOLPH** [TAG 58:136]

SAWTELL, John[2] (-bef 1700) & (only wife) Elizabeth **POST** (-1700); m bef 1691 Cambridge [REG 126:5]

SAWTELL, Jonathan[2] (1639-1690) & Mary **TARBELL** (-1676); m 3 Jul 1665 Groton [REG 126:5]

SAWTELL, Obadiah (1648-1740) & Hannah **LAWRENCE** (1661/2-1726+); m c1680 Watertown/Groton [REG 126:8]

SAWYER, John & Rebecca **(BARKER) SNOW** (-1711), w of Josiah[2] [REG 124:118]

SAYRE, Daniel[2] (-1708) m 2/wf Hannah **(WHITE) TOPPING** w of Thomas; m Southampton, LI [TAG 38:226]

SCOTTOW, John & Rebecca ( ), m2 Caleb **CHURCH** [TAG 60:135]

SEARS, Richard (not Robert) & Bathsheba **HARLOW**; m 21 Oct 1696 Plymouth, MA [TAG 60:160]

SELMAN, John & Mary **WATERS** (c1633-1717); m2 John **DOLLING**; m bef 1684 Boston [TAG 47:160]

SENDALL, Samuel[1] & Elizabeth **(DANSON) WARREN** (c1643-1727), w of John[1], m3 John **HAYWARD**, m4 Phineas **WILSON** [TAG 47:19]

SHARP, Nathaniel (1644-) & Rebecca **MARSHALL**; m 30 Dec 1668 (not 1658) Salem [RCA]

SHAW, John & Alice **PHILLIPS**; m bef 24 Apr 1674 Weymouth, MA [TAG 38:72]

SHEPARD, Israel[2] (c1650s-1719+) & _____ ; m bef 1682 Taunton/ Nansemond Co., VA [ASBO, p.372]

SHEPARD, Samuel[2] (by 1650-1707) & Mary **(PAGE) DOW** (bp 1646-1717/18); m 14 July 1673 Haverhill [ASBO, p.372]

SHEPARD, Solomon[2] (c1650s-1731) & Sarah **(EASTMAN) FRENCH** (1655-1748); w of Joseph; m 4 August 1684 Salisbury [ASBO, p.374]

SHEPARD, Thomas & 1/wf Margaret **TUTVILLE**; m 23 Jul 1632 Bossall, North Riding, Yorkshire [RCA]

SHERMAN, Edmund (1572-1641) & Joan _____ (not MAKIN); m c1598 Eng [TAG 61:79]

SHERMAN, John (bp 1585-1615/6) & Grace RAVENS (c1591-1662); m2 Thomas ROGERS; m 26 Sep 1611 Wattisfield, co Suffolk [TAG 62:76]

SHRIMPTON, Samuel & Elizabeth ROBERTS; m 12 May 1670 Boston [NGSQ 63:200]

SHUTE, Michael (-1706) & Mary RAINSFORD (not VERMAY) (1662/3-1707+); m bef 1681 Boston [REG 139:304]

SLASON, John^3 & Mary^3 HOLMES (delete CLASON entry); m 12 Jan 1692 Stamford [TAG 43:41]

SMITH, Adam^2 (c1649-) & Elizabeth BROWN; m bef 1688 Smithtown [Smith, p.48]

SMITH, Christopher & Sarah _____; m bef Oct 1655 Northampton [Pynchon Court Record, pp.389-90]

SMITH, Henry^3 (c1673-) & Rebecca_____; m c1698 [RCA]

SMITH, John^1 (1659-1727) & Mary ELLINGWOOD (1664-1750); m bef 1686 [TAG 61:7]

SMITH, Richard^1 (-1692) & Sarah ?HAMMOND (not FOLGER) (-1707+) [NYGBR 121:21]

SMITH, Richard & 2/wf Elizabeth WADE; m c1691 Lyme [TAG 49:209]

SMITH, Robert & Deborah (PRINCE) KING; w of William; m 12 Jul 1694 Boston [TAG 59:232]

SMITH, Samuel^2 (c1654-) & Hannah PERRING [RCA]

SNOW, Josiah^3 (-1692) & Rebecca BARKER (-1711); m2 John SAWYER 1694; m c1669 Marshfield [REG 124:118]

SNOW, Nicholas (not PRENCE) & Lydia SHAW; m 4 Apr 1689 Eastham/Harwich [TAG 60:160; MD 3:180; MD 4:207]

SOAN, William (-1671) & Dorothy _____; m bef 1668 Scituate [TAG 59:83]

SOMES, Morris (c1603-4-1688/9) & 1/wf Marjorie JOHNSON (-1646/7); m 4 June 1635 Cranfield, Bucks/Gloucester [TAG 53:12]

SOULE, John (-1707) & 2/wf Hester ( ) SAMPSON; m 1675-8 Duxbury [TAG 60:160; TG 1:233]

SOWTHER, Nathaniel (c1592-1655) & 1/wf Alice DEVONPORT (-1651); m 28 Mar 1613 St. Peters, Derby/Boston [TAG 42:218]

SOWTHER, Nathaniel (c1592-1655) & 2/wf Sarah (JURDAIN) HILL, w of William; m3 Edmund GREENLEAF; m 5 11mo 1653 Boston [TAG 42:218]

SPENCER, William[1] (1601-1640) & Agnes[1] HARRIS (bp 1604-1680+); m2 William EDWARDS; m bef 1633 Cambridge, MA [TAG 63:41]

SPRAGUE, John (c1635-1677) & Ruth BASSETT (1635-1693/4+) m2 ___ THOMAS; m c1655 Plymouth [TAG 41:179]

SQUIRE, Luke & Margaret STUBBS (c1660s-1709/10); Hull [REG 143:333]

STANLEY, Daniel[1] & Joan _____, m2 Thomas[1] PINSON [TAG 50:97]

STAPLES, John[2] (1647-1692) & Sarah ATKINS (c1651/2-c1724); m2 Samuel GURNEY; m3 Richard WILLIAMS; m c1670 Weymouth/Boston [REG 121:243]

STEBBINS, John (c1611-1681) & 1/wf Ann MUNKE (c1630-1680); m 17 Apr 1644 Roxbury [TAG 41:95]

STEBBINS, Martin (c1589-1657) & 2/wf Jane GREEN (-1659); m 25 Dec 1639 Roxbury [TAG 41:95]

STERLING, Daniel & Elizabeth SAWTELL (1638-bef 1692); m bef 1665 Watertown/Groton [REG 126:4]

STEVENS, John[2] (1650-1725) & Mary[2] CHASE (1650/1-1724/5+); m 9 Mar 1669/70 Newbury [ASBO, p.173]

STICKNEY, William[1] (1592-1665) & Elizabeth DAWSON (1608-1678+); m 29 Nov 1628 Cottingham, Yorks/Rowley [REG 139:319]

STOCKBRIDGE, Charles (c1634-1683) & Abigail EAMES (-1709/10); m2 Nathaniel TURNER; m c1657 Scituate [TAG 38:186]

STOCKBRIDGE, John[1] (c1608-1657) & Anne KENDALL (c1613/14-); m 16 Jan 1631/2 Rayleigh, co Essex/Scituate [NGSQ 74:111]

STOUGHTON, Samuel & Dorothy (BISSELL) WATSON (1665-1712+), w of Nathaniel[2] [REG 123:279]

STRANGE, John & Alice FEERE; m 2 Feb 1643 Ware, Herts [TAG 56:149]

STREET, Robert & Elizabeth HARKER, bef 1680s Boston [Suffolk Deed 12:282]

STUARD, Hugh & Watestill DENNE; m c1672? Falmouth/Yarmouth [TAG 60:160]

SWAN, Henry & Joan[2] RUCK, m2 George HALSEY, m3 Henry[1] FARNHAM [TAG 62:35]

SWEET, Henry[3] (-1728) & Mary ANDREW (1664-1752), m 1681 East Greenwich [TAG 52:20]

SWEET, James[3] (?1623-) & Mary GREENE (1633-), m 1653 Providence [TAG 53:29]

SWEET, John[1] & 2/wf Mary _____; m2 Ezekiel HOLLIMAN; m bef 1620 Providence [TAG 53:29]

SWEET, John[2] & 2/wf Elizabeth _____; m2 _____ WILSON; m bef 1635 Warwick [TAG 53:29]

TAINTOR, Joseph & Mary EIRE, m c1642 Watertown [TAG 65:21]

TAYLOR, Edward (-1701) & Mary MERKS (-1705); m 19 Feb 1663 Barnstable [TAG 47:229]

TAYLOR, Henry[1] (-1719) & 1/wf Mary _____ [NYGBR 120:27]

TAYLOR, Henry[1] (-1719) & 2/wf Sarah PALMER (1666-), m2 Benjamin FIELD; m 1686 Boston/NYC [NYGBR 120:27]

TAYLOR, Jacob[2] (1670-bef 1750/1) & Rebecca WEEKS (-1716+); m 29 May 1693 Barnstable [NGSQ 61:110]

THOMAS, William & Susanna ( ) ROGERS (-1677), w of Robert [REG 140:204]

THOMAS, _____ & Ruth (BASSETT) SPRAGUE (1635-1693/4+), w of John [TAG 41:179]

THURSTON, Thomas (c1610/11-) & Margaret _____; m c1631 Wrentham, Eng/Dedham [TAG 54:177]

TILLEY, Edward (1588-1621) Agnes COOPER (-1621); m 20 June 1614 Henlow, Beds/Plymouth, MA [TAG 52:198]

TING, William (-1653) & 2/wf Elizabeth COYTMORE (-bet 1642/3-6); m by 1638 Boston/Braintree [NGSQ 69:115]

TING, William[1] & 3/wf Jane ( ) HUNT (-1652); w Richard; m bet 1643-6 Eng [NGSQ 69:115]

TIPPING, Bartholomew & _____ DEAN; m bef 1685/6 Taunton [TAG 59:229]

TOMLINS, Timothy (-1645-7) & Elizabeth SPENCER; m bef 1645 Lynn [TAG 41:111]

TOPPING, Josiah (1663-1726) & Hannah SAYRE; m Southold, LI [TAG 38:227]

TOPPING, Thomas & Hannah WHITE, m2 Daniel[2] SAYRE [TAG 38:226]

TRANTOR, Thomas & Ann (BOURNE) BAILEY; w of John; m bef 1688 Freetown [TAG 40:33]

TREBBY, Peter[1] (c1638-1713/14) & 1/wf Bethiah[2] SHEPARD (c1650-1675); m c1668 Newport [ASBO, p.372]

TRENT, Mathias & Mary SMITH (1627-) dau of Richard[1]; m after 1645 [TAG 46:137]

TUCKER, Andrew[1] (c1642-1691) & Mary[2] BRIMBLECOM (bp 1646/7-); m c1663 Marblehead [DCD]

TURNER, Ezekiel & Elizabeth STARTER; m 30 Sep 1698 St Mary Magdalen, Bermondsey, London/Boston [REG 141:151]

TURNER, Israel[3] & Sarah STOCKBRIDGE, m2 Thomas[3] PINSON [TAG 50:99]

TURNER, John[1] & ____; m bef 1612 Eng/Lynn [REG 123:33]

TURNER, John[2] (c1655-65-1728) & Hannah BRETT (-1728); m c1685 Bridgewater [TAG 61:131]

TURNER, Nathaniel (1638-1715) & 2/wf Abigail (EAMES) STOCKBRIDGE (-1709/10), w of Charles; m after 1680/1 Scituate [TAG 38:186]

TYLER, Lazarus (c1661-6-) & Mary _____ (-1732); m c1687 Portsmouth, RI/Preston [TAG 52:221; 60:160]

VAIL, Jeremiah (-1687) & m2 Mary (?**FOLGER**) **PAINE**; m 24 May 1660 Southold [TAG 38:183]

VERIN, Philip (-c1649) & Dorcas _____ (-1668+); m by 1605 Eng/Salem [REG 131:100]

VERIN, Robert[2] (bp 1606-bef 1639) & Jane **CASH**; m?2 Francis **PERRY**; m 15 July 1626 St Thomas, Wilts/Salem [REG 131:102]

VIALL, Jonathan[2] (c1675-1724) & Mercy **SYLVESTER** (-1724+); m c1699 Barrington, RI [TAG 42:158]

VINAL, John & Elizabeth **BAKER** (bp 1644-); m 2 Feb 1663/4 Scituate [TAG 39:41; REG 142:123]

VINAL, John[3] & Mary **WOODWORTH**; m bef 19 Dec 1691 Plymouth [REG 142:123 & TAG 39:41]

VINSON, Nicholas & Elizabeth _____; m bef 1657 Manchester [EQC 2:50; 4:216]

VITTUM/VITTOON, John (-1712/13) & Jane _____ (-1788); m bef 1693 Scarborough/Greenland [GFS]

WADE, Robert & Susanna **BIRCHARD** (bp 1626-); Norwich/ Saybrook/Martha's Vineyard [TAG 51:18]

WALKER, Richard & Sarah **HUSTON**; m bef 29 Mar 1698 Newbury [REG 144:54]

WALKER, Samuel (-1696) & Sarah **HUNTER** (1663-1704-8); m2 Matthew **PAULING**; m c1678 Boston [TAG 40:82]

WALLEY, John[2] & Sarah[3] **BLOSSOM** (1646-50-); m c1671 Boston [TAG 63:239]

WANTON, Edward (-1716) & 2/wf Mary **PHILLIPS**; m 25 7mo 1676 Scituate [TAG 60:160]

WARD, Henry (bef 1647-c1684) & Mary **DYRE** (bef 1650-bet 1679-84); m bet 1670-78 Newport/NY/Delaware [REG 145:22-8]

WARMAN, William (c1650-c1741) & Abigail **LAY** (c1650-bef 1721); m 3 Aug 1687 Lyme [TAG 48:13; 60:160]

WARREN, John[1] (-1677) & 3/wf Elizabeth **DANSON** (c1643-1727); m2 Samuel[1] **SENDALL**; m3 John **HAYWARD**; m4 Phineas **WILSON**; m early 1670s Boston [TAG 47:19]

WASSELBE, Samuel & Bridget PLAYFER, m2 Thomas OLIVER; m 13 Apr 1660 St. Mary-in-the-Marsh, Norwich, co Norfolk [TAG 64:207]

WATSON, John & 2/wf Elizabeth[2] FROST (bp 1614-bef 1682); m 24 June 1634 St. Peter's Church, Nottingham [TAG 64:163]

WATSON, Nathaniel[2] (1663/4-1690) & Dorothy[3] BISSELL (1665-1712+); m2 Samuel STOUGHTON; m 21 Jan 1685 Windsor [REG 123:279]

WAY, Richard (bp 1624-1697) & 2/wf Bethia (MAYHEW) HARLOCK, dau Thomas & Jane; w of Thomas; m bef 1689 Boston [TAG 61:256]

WEAVER, Thomas & Mary SPRINGER; m bef 1682 RI [NGSQ 73:38]

WELD, Thomas[1] (1595-1660) & 3/wf Margaret _____ (-bef 1671); m bef 1660 [TAG 55:147]

WESTON, Elnathan[2] (c1657-1729) & Jane _____ (-1735); m by 1688 Duxbury [NGSQ 71:43]

WESTON, John[2] (c1662-1736) & 1/wf Deborah ?DELANO (c1672-bef 1717); m c1695-7 Duxbury/Plympton [NGSQ 71:44]

WHALE, Philemon (bp 1599-1675/6) & 1/wf Elizabeth (FROST) RICE (c1585-1647); w of Henry; m 24 Jan 1621/2 St Mary's Bury St Edmonds, co Suffolk/Sudbury [TG 6:131]

WHAPLES, Thomas[2] & 1/wf Rebecca GILLETTE (1657-bef 1698); m bef Mar 1687/8 Simsbury/Windsor [TAG 56:134]

WHEELOCK, Ralph[1] & Rebecca CLARKE; m 17 May 1630 Wramplingham, co Norfolk/Dedham [NGSQ 74:4]

WHELDEN, Jonathan[3] (1658-1743) & Mercy TAYLOR (1671-1742); m 1 Dec 1698 Yarmouth [TAG 48:8; 60:160]

WHITE, Paul (-1679) & Ann (PRIDDETH) (WOOD) JONES; w of Richard; w of Thomas; m 14 Mar 1664/5 Newbury [REG 139:141]

WHITE, Sylvanus[3] (-1688) & Deborah[2] CHURCH? (1657-); m bef 1683 Scituate [TAG 40:101, 60:131]

WHITE, William (-1621) & Susanna _____ (-1680); m2 Edward WINSLOWE (not husband of Ann FULLER) [TAG 60:160]

WHITTAMORE, Lawrence[1] (-1644) & Elizabeth ( ) ADAM (-1643); m 25 Feb 1627/8 Great Amwell, co Herts/Roxbury [REG 132:23]

WILKINS, Bray[1] (1611-1702) & Hannah[2] ?WAY not GINGILL; m c1636 Salem [TAG 60:3]

WILKINS, Henry[2] (c1651-1737) & 1/wf Rebecca ?BAXTER (?1648/9-   ); m c1672 Dorchester/Salem [TAG 60:103]

WILLARD, John & Margaret[3] WILKINS (c1667-1751); m2 William[3] TOWNE; m c1687 Topsfield [TAG 60:16]

WILLETT, Nathaniel & 3/wf Eleanor WATTS; m aft 1677 Hartford [TAG 46:136]

WILLIAMS, Joseph & Lydia SOMES (1649-1689-90); m bef 1670 Boston [TAG 53:13]

WILLIAMS, Nathaniel & Mary (   ); m2 Peter[1] BRACKETT [TAG 52:73]

WILLIAMS, Robert & Margery ROUND (1648-   ); m 2 June 1671 Yarmouth [TAG 54:37]

WILLIAMSON, Michael/Moyles (c1605-1645) & Ann PANKHURST (c1619-   ), m2 Henry PEARSALL; m c1638 Boston/Hempstead [NYGBR 119:81]

WILLIS, Henry (1628-1714) & Mary PEACE (c1632-1714); Warminster, Wilts/Westbury [NYGBR 118:65]

WILLIS, Richard & Patience BONHAM, m2 John[2] HOLMES [NGSQ 74:87]

WILLOUGHBY, Francis (bp 1615-1671) & 1/wf Mary TAYLOR (-1640); m 26 Nov 1635 Blackwall, Eng [TAG 56:12; 60:160]

WILSON, James (1673-1705/6) & Alice (SABEERE) HUBBARD (-1734), dau of Stephen; m c1690s Kingstown, RI [REG 144:296]

WILSON, Samuel & Mary GRIFFEN, m2 Anthony HOSKINS [TAG 52:80]

WING, Elisha (1669-1757) & Mehitable BUTLER (c1670-1731); m 12 Mar 1689 Sandwich [REG 127:24]

WINSLOW, Gilbert (1673-   ) & Mercy SNOW (1675-   ); m 7 Feb 1698 Marshfield [REG 124:119]

WOLCOTT, William & Alice[3] INGERSOLL (bp 1612-1644+); m c1630 Sandy, Bedford/Salem/Newfoundland [Abel Lunt, p.65]

WOOD, Edmund (c1585-90-   ) & Martha LOME; m 21 May 1611 Halifax/Hempstead [NYGBR 120:6]

WOOD, Edward[1] (bp 1598-1642) & Ruth LEE (-1642); m 2 Feb 1619/20 Nuneaton, co Warwick/Charlestown [TG 9:90]

WOOD, Obadiah[3] (1652/3-1712) & 1/wf Catherine KING; Hartford [TG 9:102]

WOOD, Richard & Ann PRIDDETH, m2 Thomas JONES, m3 Paul WHITE [REG 139:141]

WOOD, William & Abigail _____; m 1698 Hampstead, NY [TAG 39:140]

WOODIN, John[1] & 2/wf Mary[2] JOHNSON (-bef 1692); m bef 1653 Hampton [TAG 64:70]

WOODIN, John[1] & 3/wf Mary _____ (c1640-   ); m bef 1692 [TAG 64:70]

WORTHEN, George[3] (1669-1721+) & Anne[2] ANNIS (1681-1726+); m by 1699 Amesbury [ASBO, p.125]

YELLINGS, Roger & Elizabeth (BALLENTINE) GREENLAND, w of David, m3 John COOMBS [TAG 46:130]

Delete Roger MOWRY & 1/wf Elizabeth _____ [TAG 44:234]

delete Mary ___ m ___STERLING [REG 126:4]